Mom says no Girlfriend

Mom says no Girlfriend

Subhasis Das

Rupa & Co

Copyright © Subhasis Das 2010

Published 2010 by
Rupa Publications India Pvt. Ltd.
7/16, Ansari Road, Daryaganj,
New Delhi 110 002

Sales Centres:
Allahabad Bengaluru Chandigarh Chennai
Hyderabad Jaipur Kathmandu
Kolkata Mumbai

All rights reserved.
No part of this publication may be reproduced, stored in a retrieval system, or transmitted, in any form or by any means, electronic, mechanical, photocopying, recording or otherwise, without the prior permission of the publishers.

The author asserts the moral right to be identified as the author of this work.

Typeset by
Mindways Design
1410 Chiranjiv Tower
43 Nehru Place
New Delhi 110 019

Printed at Repro Knowledgecast Limited, Thane

Dedicated to all the women in my life.

Contents

Acknowledgements	*ix*
Hello	1
Hyderabad Blues	3
My first crush	12
Mamma's boy	24
I still remember	32
Meeting Mr Legend	42
My first sex	51
Staying away	60
My first affair	69
It's all over	79
The Failure	88

Adding a new chapter	97
He is back	104
Corporate Culture	115
The Birthday Girl	123
The End and the Beginning	136
The daddy's girl	146
My first romance	159
The Betrayal	169
Life with Pogo	177
The Success	188
She is back	198
I love you	209
The Empathy and the Selfishness	223
I love you too	233

Acknowledgements

Thank you very much ...

Baba and Ma for being the best parents though I know I have not been the best son! Sorry for my ATKTs, night-outs, low attendance and all the other things which have made you unhappy and sad. My Dadu, Dida and all my family members. I feel really blessed to have such a caring and supportive family.

My two best friends—Ajay and Sudeep, for being with me and for supporting me through thick and thin. Misbah, Samarth and Ujjwal for their unstinted support during my college years.

And the ladies ...

Tanushree, the girl who is and will always continue to be my best friend. Thank you for giving me the best moments of my life. You made me realise and understand my own mistakes. Miss Jabalpur ... for being a complete sweetheart. Rashmi, for still being so kind to me after all those pranks and tantrums I played upon to irritate you! I wish you a happy life in America. Namita, for making me realise that not all girls are as stupid as boys perceive them to be and how can I forget the beautiful song you sang for me on my birthday. Joyeta and Shivani for being my oldest friends. Ashwini and Righu for giving me company in my lonely days.

Debashree, Indrani, and Prachi ... my sweet online friends.

Sanchita, Sapna, Shefali, Shubhra and Urmi for leaving behind trails after their guest appearances in my life.

Monu didi and Christina di for letting me always eat their brains and digest their advises which never sustained!

Priti Sharma Joshi, my first boss. I wish I knew where you are now. I really owe a lot to you.

All my colleagues at my first workplace and my other friends ...

Usama for helping me with the poetry part. A special thanks to Mr Anonymous, Anubhav and Ruchi for sending me my first fan mails.

Rupa & Co. for the interest shown in my work and also for their suggestions and guidelines throughout the process. A special thanks to Hemambika Varma for editing my work and more importantly for tolerating me over the months.

Lastly, my sincere thanks to my Lappy (laptop) for saving and supporting all my (corrupt) files!!

Hello

'Hello, aunty ... it's Shalini here', said Shalini.

'Oh! Hi ... but Somu is not here,' my Mom replied rather curtly.

'I know, he is not there. And, why should he be there, he must be basking in some exquisite holiday spot ...' [*Only Shalini had the guts to speak like that to Mom!*]

'Really ...? It seems this time you missed the bus!' My Mom replied rather tongue-in-cheek. Although she was a little surprised at Shalini's remark, she was happy to learn that Shalini no longer existed for me.

'How cheap of you Aunty ... why should I be accompanying him? But it did hurt that he kept me in the dark about it ...' Shalini replied.

'I can understand *beta*. I know, my son is wrong. But then whatever happens is for a good cause, maybe there is something really great lined up for you. Try to take it in that manner. You both need to think beyond each other, the world is full of good people. Be a bit practical,' my Mom tried to reason with her.

A bit taken aback by my Mom's explanation, Shalini replied, 'Does being practical mean not to invite best friends on your wedding ... having a relation with one and getting married to somebody else ... I guess ... that's how your son treats people who love him.' Shalini gave the heat back to Mom.

'Whose wedding are you talking of?' My mom retorted rather shockingly. She had her heart almost in her mouth.

'Ma'am, I am speaking about your "practical" son Somu's wedding. Now you understand why I called him mean,' Shalini replied.

My Mom was devastated over the news; she sat still on the sofa for a while till she regained her senses.

'Hello ... Hello ... Aunty ... are you fine? Please, say something ... Hello ...' Shalini kept yelling hard.

'Yes ... yes ... *beta* I am all right. I am as disturbed as you ... I ... I really don't know what to say ... he didn't even tell me once,' Mom said recollecting herself.

'Does that mean Somu didn't invite his own Mom? Oh! He is really sick, Aunty,' Shalini went on cursing me while Mom hung up to call me.

Hyderabad Blues

'Wow! This is really nice ... a TV ... an air-conditioner ... and that little lamp there ...', I said as we entered the room. I tried hard so as to not show my nervousness.

She removed her coat and relaxed on the bed.

'What ... are you thinking?' I asked her as she continued to stare at me.

'What am I thinking ... what sort of a question is this?' She snapped at me.

'I am sorry ... I don't know,' I replied rather sheepishly, acting as innocent as I could, waiting for her to take the initiative.

She rose on her knees ... unbuttoned her top ... I watched her all the while.

'Come here', she gestured towards me. My hands reached for her blonde silky hair but ...

Blonde ...? Does that mean I am with a *videshi kudi* ... *an outlander?* I was sure, it was a dream and instantly opened my eyes.

And I was right, it was indeed a dream, where else I would get a chance to be with ELISHA CUTHBERTH. (The sexiest porn star)!

∞

I adjusted the pillow and lifted my head to have a look around; last night had been pretty long and wild, I realised. An empty champagne bottle lay on the floor, clothes were strewn all over; in short the place looked completely untidy.

'Good morning,' said Nandini who lay next to me. Before I could respond my phone started ringing ... a call from Mom. I took the call and gestured Nandini to be quiet.

'Good morning, Mom.' I greeted.

'Morning ...? Check the time, the sun is already over your head,' Mom said angrily.

'Mom ... it's my off today,' I replied.

'Liar ... don't lie to me. I very well know what you are up to behind my back.'

I was shocked by Mom's answer. How the hell could she have known what I was up to! Was she aware of my sleeping stints and one night stands? No ways ... I tried to think rationally ... I could sense that Mom was disturbed. Her voice became heavy; it seemed that she was crying.

I tried reasoning out with her, 'Mom, see I can explain ... I tried to defend myself.'

'What ... will you explain to me now? You are my only child, I had so many dreams for you ... but then you never cared for me,' she sobbed.

'What exactly are you talking of Mom?' I was confused. There was something going wrong, I knew.

I repeated 'Mom, can you clear what exactly you are talking about?'

'What do I have to clear ... my son didn't even think of informing me before getting married ...' her voice crumbled and she started sobbing.

'What? So, now I get it what the sudden *hungama* was all about,' I heaved a sigh of relief and said a secret prayer ... Thank God! My Mom knew nothing of my secret adventures.

'MOM', I screamed ... 'I am in Hyderabad for some official work ... damn!'

'Oh! ... I ... I ...', my Mom didn't know what to say.

'How could you even think that way Mom? It's disgusting', I snapped at her.

'Somu ... Somu ... please, let me explain,' there was a relief in my Mom's voice now.

'I knew my son will never cheat me. Your friend Shalini is a liar. You better cut off from her completely now. She almost gave me a minor stroke ...' Mom continued doing what she does best, cursing Shalini. I didn't stop her either.

'Look Mom, forget it. I would never do anything wrong to defame your name. Okay ... I think I had enough of it for today ... I am keeping the phone down,' I said.

'Okay beta ... I am sorry for everything ... bye ... but I hope you are not hiding anything,' my Mom checked for the last time.

Unable to bear the *emotional atyachar* any longer, I shouted back 'Mom, just shut up or else I would stop taking your calls and I really mean it.'

The threat always worked and I never shied using it. And, the best part is Mom knows that I don't lie to her but then ... what she doesn't know is that ... I never tell the truth either.

'I swear Mom, nothing has happened, please believe me.'

'Okay ... I believe you', she said.

'Okay then, Mom,' I said and hung up.

I checked my phone; there were fifteen missed calls, thirteen from Shalini and two from Pogo. I dialled Shalini but was in no mood to talk to her, and I knew the most she would do is hurl abuses at me. Thereby, I disconnected the call and switched off my phone to avoid Shalini.

I looked around and was a little shocked to see Nandini draped in a towel. I couldn't help but stare at her.

Seeing me stare she snapped at me, 'What ... I just took my bath ... why are you staring like that?'

I got up from the bed to hug Nandini who was combing her long curly hair. She smiled at me; I kissed on her shoulder only to notice a love bite which bought back the memories of the romp session I had with her last night. I held her in my arms to kiss her ... but there was a knock at the door! Somebody was at the door.

'It must be the waiter, you keep waiting here sweetie, I will be back in a flash.' I shot at her and ran to answer the bell. As I opened the door slightly, I was stunned to see Subho, one of my fans. But before I could respond or acknowledge him he pushed me and eased himself in. Nandini was still standing (in towel) and stood there more in shock, unable to reckon what was happening and what to do on seeing Subho.

'This is Subho, my friend,' I introduced but she rushed to the bathroom. I shrugged at Subho and he did the same. I sat on the bed and he on the chair, both of us remained silent. He too looked a little embarrassed.

Nandini sneaked out of the bathroom; Subho had his back, while I was facing her. She gestured something to me, which I didn't understand, I shrugged with confusion.

'I think she wants her clothes.' Subho suggested, seeing me doing strange things.

'Wow! You're really smart, thank you very much,' I said and pushed some of her stuffs in. The silence gripped the room once again; I don't know how long it takes to roll on jeans and put on a t-shirt but that day, Nandini chose not to come out of the bathroom as long as Subho was there. Subho somehow understood the fact and rose to go.

'Wrong timing ... I am sorry sir,' Subho said and walked to the door.

'It's okay ...' I comforted him. 'Leave aside everything; tell me how come, you are in Hyderabad?'

'Industrial visit, Sir,'.

'Okay, then I will catch up with you some other time ... bye,' I said and escorted him to the door.

Nandini was still inside the bathroom, I yelled at her to come out. When she did, she made my heart literally take off. She was looking stunning in a purple top and a white long skirt. I was mesmerised by her personality and lost myself completely; she had to shake me to wake me up.

'Stop staring at me, Sam,' she blushed.

'Do you know something, you are looking so beautiful today,' I said as I got a bit closer to her but she drew me away.

'God damn, it's enough Sam,' she pushed me aside.

'Coming to the point, who was he?' She asked.

I couldn't control myself from laughing recalling the scene but Nandini was serious and gave me a furious *shut-up* look.

'Okay ... okay ... cool ... I didn't think he would just barge in. I am sorry. He's a fan of mine. I met him during one of my concerts. He is on an industrial visit tour,' I said

'Anyway, I have some work. I'll catch up with you for lunch at Kamat, first floor and don't you dare come late,' said Nandini and left.

It was 11.30 a.m. which meant I still had three hours before I meet her again for lunch and so I moved around at my own pace. I knew Nandini liked those typical gentleman-type guys. So I shaved, gelled my hair to get a formal look and wore a suit to be the most decent chap at the restaurant.

After I finished dressing up, I looked at my watch; I still had an hour more to meet Nandini. I switched on my cell and instantly my phone vibrated; a message from Shalini, it read:

'You bloody coward, pick up my phone. I will kill you, ass**** if we cross each other ever. You and your friendship just fuck off.'

I instantly understood everything—the outburst must have been because of my Mom. I ignored the message and dialled to call Pogo instead.

'Hi there, what's up, buddy?' I greeted. 'How was your journey?'

'It was long and tiring. How about you ... first tell me how is she?' Pogo questioned.

'She is really awesome. Her name is Nandini.'

'Wow! So, did you propose her?'

'No ... no ... not so soon, my friend. I have to be sure of her. We just met yesterday. I mean ... would she have loved me this way, if I weren't popular.'

'Can't say *yaar*, you know *na*, I know nothing about girls,' he said and we both had a hearty laugh.

After a long chat, I hung up finally. I looked at my watch. I still had some time left yet preferred to leave so that I reach first. Yet, somehow I was not able to make it, Nandini was already there waiting for me.

'Actually, I had a meeting here and it just got over. I was thinking of reading some book but it seems you respect time, I appreciate that. Thank you, you saved me from getting bored,' Nandini said and rose to give me a hug but I planted a kiss on her cheeks.

Slightly taken aback by my behaviour, Nandini reminded me, 'Dear, it's a restaurant. I hope you realise it.'

Trying to conceal my goof, I pulled out a chair for her and said 'Please, have a seat madam.'

'What's wrong with you?' Nandini asked.

'I guess that's what gentlemen do when they meet gentlewomen ... Oops! I mean ... you know what I meant,' I fumbled.

'What? Who told you that?'

'Pogo.'

Nandini thought for a while after hearing the name.

'Well, tell me frankly. Is there really nothing between you and him?'

'Come on, Nandini, how could you even think like that? He's my best friend; is there anything wrong with that?' I snapped at her.

'No ... no ... it's not like that Sam; you always talk about him, you measure all people against him to see if they're your material and practically share almost everything under the Sun with him; so I just pondered if he was ever more than a friend to you,' Nandini justified.

'You think I am a gay?' Maybe my voice or the word is so 'popular' that it turned a few heads in the restaurant towards us.

'Sorry,' I apologised.

'It's okay ... but believe me you're looking quiet decent today. I am impressed,' she said toasting her glass.

'Oh! Really, I am trying too hard for you,' I held her hand. 'I broke my own rules ... otherwise I shave only on Sundays. I wouldn't have done this even for Pogo.' I bit my tongue and looked at her, I was caught.

'See,' she smiled and said 'I love you, Sam ... when are you going to propose to me?'

'Well, I haven't thought of it yet, I mean we need to give each other some more time; we just met yesterday.'

'Oh! Really,' she said rather sarcastically with a sly smile.

'And this thought didn't strike your mind when you slept with me last night ... all men are bastards,' she replied angrily.

'And you women enjoy being fucked by bastards,' I replied rather tongue-in-cheek.

My timing was again wrong; Nandini gave me a very nasty look at my comment. She got even more furious and none of us said anything for the next few seconds. I was wondering what to do to relax her when Subho came in as a saving grace for me.

'Good afternoon, sir,' Subho greeted. 'It seems Hyderabad is a very small city. Here we meet again.'

'Oh ... Hi! Nice to see you again, please have a seat,' I offered him a seat which to my surprise he willingly accepted.

'Sir, you had promised to invite me on your marriage but ...' he said looking at Nandini.

'See, I am not his wife. You are mistaken. We are just *gooood* friends,' Nandini corrected him in a rather rude way.

'Yeah! She is Nandini ...' I was unable to recollect her last name.

'The name is Mehra, Nandini Mehra,' she said getting even more serious.

'Wow! That's Bond style. Nice name, Madam,' Subho replied to which Nandini smiled.

'Thank you ... I guess it's not Sam's mistake either. We met only yesterday' said Nandini, swirling the straw in her drink.

Subho's creative mind pondered as he heard that and recollected the morning scene. I could guess his conclusions. Trust a girl to come up with something as foolish as this. It's rightly said that girls have their brains on their knees.

'Nandini, our Subho is a writer. He has even authored a novel,' I tried to change the topic.

'Really, what do you write about?' Nandini asked.

'I love to write about romance,' Subho answered.

'Then, you can do a PhD. on Sam, I tell you he is a living legend.'

'That's a good joke,' I interrupted 'But yeah! I do have many stories to share and would definitely narrate it to you once any of the stories get a happy ending.'

'I will wait for it sir,' answered Subho. 'Anyways ... when is your next album releasing?'

'Next month.'

'Oh, great! I will definitely buy an original CD and not download it!' He paused to look at the time and said, 'I need to go now or else Gautami madam, I mean Sridevi would kill me.'

'Hey, is that character real?' I asked.

'What do you think ... bye,' he smiled and left.

'Who is Gautami ... err ... Sridevi?' Nandini asked.

'She is his teacher, and she is a lesbian,' I answered.

'What? Not again,' Nandini blushed.

'Oh, come on Nandini, he had written about her in his book. 'Anyway, I am sorry Nandini,' I held her hand. 'I love you. I might have proposed to you right now but ...'

'But ... what?' Nandini looked at me anxiously.

'Waiting for the rate of gold to fall, so that I can buy a ring, you see it's over fifteen thousand rupees now.'

'Such a cheapo, you're!' her mood changed finally, I realised that as she clasped her hand over mine.

My first crush

My brain was screwed up as I was thinking about the happy ending of a story which I had promised Subho to narrate. I wondered whether I should propose Nandini or not. Does she really love me; what if I was just Samarth Sinha, would she have loved me then and more importantly, do I love her? What love? 'Not again ... Sam' (something inside me responded). On New Year's Day, I had made a resolution not to fall in love anymore. After three refusals, couple of break-ups and one betrayal, I had lost complete faith in love. So, there is no way I am buying Nandini a ring, at least not this year.

For those out there who are less experienced than me, let me tell you, like everything in this world, love also ends one day. Love is an ugly terrible business. It would tamper your heart and leave you bleeding on the floor and what does it get at the end, nothing but a few incredible memories which you could never shake off your mind.

My first crush 13

If I really had to narrate few tales of my romance, I would have to rewind twelve years backward ...

∾

It was 15 August 1997, the 50th year of Independence. Standing at the school parade, I was rather feeling very restless. I steered my eyes around to look for her, but she was nowhere. She was absent, but why and moreover how? Doesn't she realise the importance of India's 50th Independence Day, does her family not care about it at all?

'Where is she?' I asked Shalini.

'Who?'

'The new girl.'

'Hey! She is not a new girl anymore.'

Yeah! It's true she is been here for quite some time and isn't a new entrant but I liked calling her that way because she was the one who had introduced me with this new-found expression in my life that is called "love". Feeling frustrated by her absence I thought why the hell did I have to discover this ridiculous pain inside me so early because I was so happy and carefree earlier. I lived in the world of men, I was happy ... truly happy, my life was full of fun, sports and constant adventure with friends without any restrictions from Mom. And, love is such a pain that I won't wish it to happen even for my worst enemies.

∾

'Look out, you idiot, it's no hit zone there,' I shouted at Paramjeet as he hit the ball over the wall of the neighbouring building. It's not that I was worried that the ball hit someone there but the rules said I had to cross the LoC, enter the enemy territory and fetch the ball.

14 Mom says no Girlfriend

My plan was simple as I climbed over the wall, sneak in quietly, get the ball and run to safety as soon as possible. But where was the ball? I poached in further and after ten minutes of serious searching, I finally got my target. I picked up the ball and turned only to realise that I was caught, they had surrounded me from all sides, and there was no way to escape. I didn't dare to raise my head to count how many were there.

'What are you doing here?' The interrogation started.

'Actually, our ball came to your side,' I replied.

'Leave him, he's just a kid.'

'Hey, how dare you call me that?' I snapped at them and my sight was caught by a lovely girl in pink dress. Wow! Who was she ... I have never seen her before.

'Stop!' I shouted. 'I am going.'

That night I couldn't sleep, all I was thinking was about her. And ... I didn't even know her name, it was really frustrating. Well, for that I had to go to the other end once again, 'The Big Boyz' would kick me out of it if they come to know about my infatuation. But who really cares about this bloody club whose leader was, of course, that stinking Paramjeet! Whom am I kidding ... I need them lest I had to be satisfied playing *Ghar-Ghar* with Shalini all my life!

The next morning was really bad for me, the vacations were over and I had to wake up early to go to school. And, to make the day even worse, Paramjeet splashed a pool of muddy water on me with his new cycle. Oh! I felt like crying but 'Big Boyz' don't cry and don't forgive either. I punctured his cycle on reaching the school and worst was he saw me doing it.

Our fight drew a good audience; nobody stopped us instead they goaded both of us by cheering continuously. I pushed Paramjeet down on the ground while he rose and gave a punch on my face, my lips started to bleed and I kicked him hard straight on his stomach.

For a few seconds he didn't realise the pain as he lay silent on the ground but when he did, he cried loudly.

However, our teacher, Nair Ma'am was smart enough not to be carried away by his *rona-dhona*. Both of us were punished equally, our parents were called and till then we were made to stand in front of the principal's office which was really a shameful act in my school. Paramjeet was used to it and didn't mind the punishment at all; he thought it was much better than attending classes. I was silent though as I was wondering what was waiting for me back at home when my parents would be informed. But then all of a sudden ... the depression, pain and the enemy (Paramjeet) seemed to disappear the moment I saw the little angel, the girl in the pink dress, again.

I thought I was daydreaming and asked Paramjeet 'Can you pinch me?'

'Aah! I got it and you would complain to Madam, sorry I am not that dumb,' Paramjeet said.

I tell you he really had a brain similar to the ants and used it even lesser than them. Shalini always said, if ever possessing smaller brains comes in fashion, Paramjeet would be a legend.

Crap it, back on track. She was wearing a pink frock again and was looking stunning again; I sneaked in the principal's office to have a look. She was looking at the trophy cabinet while her parents were having a word with the principal; I wished she noticed last year's junior quiz competition cup; I was a part of the winning team. Well, I have this certificate at home to prove and more importantly my name too was inscribed in the trophy with others. But she didn't know my name and neither did I. I tried to peep in a bit more so that I could get my ear over what was going inside and then suddenly I felt a tap on my head.

'Paramjeet, I will kill you,' I thought but ignored it. Yet again, I got another tap, I turned violently to smack Paramjeet but thankfully I didn't; it was Nair Ma'am.

'Any problem, boys?' She asked.

'Nothing, Ma'am,' I said rather sheepishly.

'Okay, then excuse me, let me get in,' she said. I stood aside and she went in.

'Paramjeet, do you know that girl? She stays near your home. I asked him though I knew he won't answer because of the morning drama and ... I was right. Paramjeet replied, 'I told you, call me Jeet, not Paramjeet and why do you think that I would favour you?'

He's such a mean fellow, I felt like giving him a punch right there but that would impose a suspension, I was aware of that and chose to remain silent. But what's her name? That was the only thing going on in my mind then.

'Come Shamita, let me show your class,' I could hear Nair Ma'am say it.

Okay ... she is Shamita; I found the answer to my question.

'Hi!' I said with a big grin as she came outside the room.

'Do you know each other?' Nair Ma'am asked.

'Yeah! I know Jeet, he stays in our society,' she said and my heart sank. She knew the bastard, Oh! I hate him even more.

'You must be glad to know that he is in your class,' said Nair Ma'am.

'That's really good,' she lauded and I was very much disappointed at the new developments. But somehow Paramjeet didn't seem to acknowledge her at all. He was not the type to be mad after girls or fall for anyone. For that matter very few, almost negligible, would think of girls at the age of eleven. But then ... I was an exception right from the start.

'I have some work, why don't you both take her to the class,' Nair Ma'am said. It was an opportunity I was waiting for and had been secretly praying to God.

'Ma'am, aren't we supposed to stand here till our parents come, we have been punished, *na?*' Paramjeet protested.

'Thanks for your kind information, Paramjeet … okay then, Samarth, you take her to the class and Paramjeet, you enjoy yourself here.'

I grabbed the opportunity with both hands and said thanks to Jeet, 'you're a sweetheart.'

As we walked together to the class, I introduced myself; she responded with a smile but didn't mention anything of our last day's encounter. I was happy anyway to be with her.

The class had finished and our teacher hadn't arrived yet. I had my time and went up straight to the dais to introduce her.

'Well … class, this is Shamita. She will be in our class from now.' I declared and all of us in the class cheered together.

'New Kid! New Kid! …' they shouted.

'What?' Shamita asked.

I had completely forgotten about this *New Kid* tradition of my class. It's like ragging at school level. Each newcomer to the class is given the new kid tag till the class fixes up another name for the student. But at times, it has happened that we had been unable to decide upon a new name and the new 'kid tag' remained with the person for two years!

Shamita demanded an explanation from me on the 'new kid' concept. I was at a loss of words as I didn't want her to think that we were making fun of her.

'Oh! well, it's nothing. You wouldn't have to hear that for long,' I said guiltily.

'I didn't get it, Samarth,' she said looking rather confused.

'You would understand the concept soon. Don't boggle your mind over this now.'

Just before recess, the peon came to pick me up; my Mom had visited the school. I very well knew what lay in store for me, so I decided to keep my mouth shut and let Mom finish all that she wanted to say to me. There was no point in arguing or explaining anything to her then.

'How many times have I told you not to hit anyone ... Somu ... Somu ... are you listening to me?' she shouted.

'Yes, I am listening to you and stop calling me Somu, don't forget that we are in school.'

'Are you trying to argue with me? Don't change the topic ... just take your bag and come home with me,' she ordered.

At home, the situation was no better; Mom was really angry with me. Last month itself when I was again engaged in a brawl, my Grandma's sudden visit saved me from the beatings. Yet, Mom banned TV and video games for me and curbed my outing for a week. I was apprehending what my punishment would be this time.

'Mom, I said sorry ... please forgive me, let me go just for today,' I begged. Having broken the Big Boyz rule no: 3, no crying in public, Paramjeet was for sure dethroned and I had a fair chance to be his successor. However, it was impossible to make Mom agree. Dad too, had a bad day in office and I reckoned that, as I saw him entering silently hanging his head down. I milked the situation by sobbing even louder and thanks to Dad I was thrown out of home immediately.

I was the new boss of Big Boyz; it was the time for change. I kicked Spiderman out and put Batman as our new idol. Santa-Banta jokes were allowed. Beckham posters were replaced by Sachin's as our new mentor. No more football, Big Boyz would just play cricket. And finally, English music was banned. I wanted a reaction from Paramjeet but he was silent throughout his court martial.

Next day, Dad came to drop me at the school. I saw her again, getting down from a white Esteem. She was not wearing pink that day, but I tell you, nobody ever had looked so pretty in their school uniform. According to Shalini, sky blue shirt and navy blue skirt (the uniform for girls in school) sucks. But Shamita looked no less than an angel in that very uniform.

'Dad, you see that girl there ... she is a an angel,' I said.

'What ...?' Dad exclaimed. He seemed rather shocked by my comment.

'I mean ... err ... her name is Angel. She is a new entrant in our class,' I corrected myself.

'You're wrong my son, her name is Shamita ... her Dad is my new boss,' Dad said.

Wow! She was rich, too. *My future is safe if I get her!*

'Oh! I see. I don't understand then why she had to lie to me', I tried covering my guilt.

'Son, you're still small for all this.'

'What do you mean?'

'*Main tumhara baap hoon, beta,*' my Dad answered with a smile.

☙

I could see the *new kid* effect in her. She was sitting alone in the first bench, not talking to anybody, no smiles, nothing at all. I thought of giving her company but then boy—girl sitting together was a taboo in our class. So, I quickly occupied the bench behind her; the fragrance of her hair was everywhere in the room and I leaned forward to guess what shampoo could it be but couldn't recognise it.

'Rose, jasmine or *chameli* ...' I couldn't figure out.

'It's strawberry,' Shalini pinched me from the next bench.

'Strawberry ...?' I never knew it was used in shampoos also, I thought it was meant only for jams and ice-creams. I thought of saying 'hi' to her, then thought I should wait for her to initiate. Girls are shy, I hoped she was not blaming me for the 'new kid' tag. I reckoned an apology may make things better between us but then I was not sure if she would agree. And, even if she did the class wouldn't let her forget the tag.

'Good morning, class,' Nair Ma'am greeted as she entered the class with a dull boy.

'The new kid,' I shouted out of joy.

'Yes Samarth, he is your new classmate. But what's there to be so excited?' Ma'am asked. Heart of heart, I thought 'you wouldn't understand Ma'am how happy I was, on his arrival. Thank you God, again.'

○○

I didn't wait long after that to say 'hi' to her and this time she responded. Actually, I was at Shalini's place and she happened to hop there. It was not always that Shalini was miserable before me, but it was another lucky day for me. I was just a few moves away from my first win after I learnt chess from her, a year ago. I knew it was something more than a coincidence; it was an opportunity to impress Shamita.

'That's a check for the third time in a row,' I declared proudly as I moved my Queen diagonally and put it in the last corner of the black block. I looked up to see Shalini's reaction and I saw that Shamita was standing next to her and watching our game.

'Not all that good, dude,' she said and blocked my Queen with her Bishop. In the next few minutes, I saw half of my Army going down and finally she said: 'Your game is over, buddy ... checkmate,' and placed her Knight two and half blocks before my king.

'That's not possible, there should be a way out,' I exclaimed, but trust me there wasn't any. It was really CHECKMATE.

Man! I had never seen anybody so smart and beautiful too. She was just my type. Wow! I didn't even realise as to when had I started categorising myself!! The cute little angel had changed my life all over and I was completely smitten by her. My Dad would be very happy about this, I thought. For the next couple of hours that I spent with her, I realised she was a person who loved herself; she enjoyed being a topic of a chat. And that was all I needed. I got to know everything about her and she was more than happy to narrate her own tales. Hours and hours rolled over but her stories wouldn't end. Finally, her pink watch that beeped every hour reminded her that it was getting late and she should go home.

'Okay! See you then, bye ... by the way, what's your name? I am sorry ... eh ... I forgot,' she said. Oh! Come on, I had planned my whole life with you ... and you have forgotten my name? How could she be so mean? But then she was too pretty to be ignored.

In the days to come, I added more and more chapters to my romance. I did many weird things like I watched almost all the classic love stories—DDLJ, Titanic ... and the like. Still, I couldn't muster up courage to say anything to her. Watching all these movies only made me want her more.

It was 29 July, one day before her birthday (*she was eleven days elder to me, but I knew if need be, in future I could explain to Mom*). I thought of buying her a gift. I had never bought a gift for anybody before but thanks to the owner of the shop who helped me out and suggested that I buy a water bottle considering her age and more importantly, my budget. But the difficult task was still on me as I pondered over which colour to buy. I knew pink was her favourite but also the Big Boyz rule no 1: 'Hate Pink'. So, after contemplating for a while, I bought a purple one.

My efforts went all in vain as she was absent on her birthday. I tried calling her but the phone went unanswered. Desperate to meet her, I lied at home that I had been invited for Shamita's birthday and went to her home but was again disappointed when I found it locked. I hid the gift and returned home.

Two days later she returned and told me that, her parents and a few of her family friends had gone to a nearby resort to celebrate her birthday. I gave the gift I bought for her after school. She liked my gift but didn't like the colour! She said 'It would have been so nice if it were pink.' She also showed me the pink wrist band that was gifted to her by somebody. I knew I would lose her if I don't tell her soon about my feelings for her … but how?

I thought of writing all my feelings for her in a letter and give it to her.

Shalini suggested that I should hand over the letter only on my birthday. But I thought otherwise since I didn't want to propose when my parents were around. And, on my birthday I would be the centre of attraction and if Mom got a hint of it, I would be gone forever. Moreover, my letter was not ready yet. And finally, we zeroed down the date to 15 August after school.

On that day I was anxiously searching for her all over the school and was hoping that she was not absent. I found her finally; she was standing on the stage to help the teachers give away gifts to meritorious students. This task was assigned to the most prettiest and presentable girl in the school and there was no doubt as to why Shamita was chosen for the task.

I was enthralled to see her in a traditional outfit—*lehenga*. My heart thumped hard each time she walked over the stage carrying those prizes. I felt upset, since I was not on the list of winners, else, I would have also had the opportunity to receive a gift from her or maybe I could have even got a snap with her. But …!

After the function, I sneaked around secretly towards the girls' room. I was apprehensive as it would be like the most embarrassing moment if somebody caught me there. Shalini was with me for my cover. I was wondering, as I was waiting outside, what it really takes girls so long inside. Finally, I saw her coming out.

'Hey, what are you doing here?' she exclaimed out of shock.

'Nothing really … I … I came to wish you Happy Independence Day', I fumbled.

'Oh! Okay … wish you also the same.'

'Yeah! Thanks. I had got this thing for you which …' I dipped my hand in my bag for the letter but … where was it? I searched even harder and also dunk my head in but it was nowhere in the bag. I looked up and saw her staring weirdly at me.

'Sorry, I think I have forgotten to carry it. I will give it to you later,' I said sheepishly and she left. Shalini raced towards me to know what happened.

'What? You couldn't find the letter?' Shalini asked me furiously. She was keen on pairing me with Shamita because she hated Shamita and thought that if ever Shamita and I got into a relationship, I would make her (Shamita's) life miserable.

'Maybe, you have forgotten it at home,' she suggested and I prayed that I hadn't committed such a big blunder. I ran back home to check … but …!!

Mamma's boy

The Sun had gone down. It was already dark, I realised as I peeped outside the window. My palms were still paining hard and it pained even more as I opened them to look at the red rashes. Mom was really harsh on me this time. I thought of putting the lights on but was feeling too weak to do so. And then the door opened, I was sure for Mom so I hung my head down. The light was put on; it was hurting my swollen eyes and I quickly covered my face.

'Sorry ... is there a dim light?' it was Shalini.

'The second one from left', I said in a crooked voice and quickly tried to wipe my tears.

'Have some water. It may clear your throat,' she said and handed me a glass of water.

'Thank you, Shalini.'

'Don't thank me. Thank your Dad; he called me.'

'Really ...?' I sighed. I have always denied it but I knew that my Dad understands me very well.

'How could you forget the letter on the study table?' she asked.

'Well ...' I smiled at my own stupidity.

'I had drawn some symbols on the letter using water colours and had left it on the table for it to dry. In the morning, I got up late and in a hurry I forgot to put it inside my bag.

'You boys are so careless,' she commented. 'So, I guess that's the end of it.'

I nodded as that was really the end of my fantasy love story. Shalini left after some time. It was really nice of her to come and comfort me.

☙

Everybody was silent at the dinner table. I didn't dare to look into my Mom's eyes. I knew she was still furious. I had done something which she had least expected. I was guilty and couldn't eat properly. I felt like a convict whose verdict was ready to be pronounced!! I rose from the table.

'Somu ... don't you dare get up ... finish your food first,' Mom scolded.

'I can't eat. My throat is paining,' I replied with my head still down.

'It's okay, *beta*,' Dad comforted me. 'You go to your room.'

'Just leave him alone,' Dad bawled at Mom.

'It all happened because of you. You never tried to know what your son is doing ... it's just your office that you care for,' Mom blasted back on dad.

'Oh! Really, then what have you done staying at home,' Dad shouted.

'Please, you both stop it. It was all my fault.' As I said that, I was almost in tears again. I ran to my room.

Ten minutes later, I was still weeping inside my quilt. But why? I couldn't figure out what made me cry so much. I had not committed any crime. The door of my room opened and I felt somebody sitting beside me but I didn't look up.

'Hey! Why are you angry with me, I didn't even say anything to you,' it was Dad.

'I did wrong, Dad ... I am sorry,' I said.

'Mom loves you a lot, she is not wrong in reprimanding you. It's alright now. Forget about it. But tell me from where did you get the courage to think something like that?' Dad exclaimed.

'I am not sure how I got the courage. But, I liked that girl and didn't just want to remain her classmate,' I explained it to Dad.

'So, you wrote that letter,' Dad laughed. 'From where do you get such ideas ... is it from those nonsensical Hindi films?' Dad questioned.

'I don't know. I just thought I should write to her.'

'Okay, but remember, you're just eleven and not ready for all this. Just forget whatever happened, okay?' Dad advised me and I nodded in the affirmative.

'Boy! Her dad is my boss, think of me at least,' Dad joked and finally I turned to give him a tight hug ... a *jaadu ki jhappi*. It really works.

The very next day, our eyes met again. However, I ignored her completely, not because Dad was there with me but I desperately wanted to move on. It was not that easy though and l guess love never is. And after that, we both were always on different paths. We created a virtual wall between us and were happy to be on our respective sides. But then those unsaid words in the letter always suffocated me again and again. Though, there were other girls in my life later, I never could quite get over her, my first love.

It took almost a week for things to become normal between me and Mom. But what I considered normalcy was actually not normal at all. Mom became even more protective and conservative towards me. She monitored my life all the time. She curtailed my TV schedule, no movies, banned MTV, restricted my outings after dark, picked me up from school and also accompanied me to birthday parties. She tried to assert her authority on everything that included me—be it my room, my cupboard, my books or my bathroom! She was like the dictator of my life and I became the *Mamma's boy* for my friends.

ॐ

'Hey! Why do you think we are not going to the school ground?' Paramjeet rebelled and he was not alone, most of them were feeling that the society backyard was too small for us to play comfortably.

'Look, my Mom would never allow me to cross the highway just to play cricket,' I explained my situation.

'So, that's your problem. You don't come then, sit at home and cook food with your Mom.'

'Don't you dare talk like that,' I warned.

'Oh! I am so scared,' Paramjeet teased. 'What will you do now? You *Mamma's boy*.'

Paramjeet continued yelling that and everybody there too joined him. I covered my ears but yet their chants penetrated in. They all surrounded me. I tried to get off it while they pushed, pulled and dragged me inside their circle. I pounced on them to make my way. A few of them went down and I tried to escape but the rest grabbed me, I struggled to free myself and kicked whoever came in the range. They too reciprocated with punches, kicks and slaps all over and finally bang! Something hard hit my head and I collapsed on the ground.

I don't remember what happened next; Dad told me later that our watchman had carried me home. When I regained consciousness, I realised that I was in the hospital. Two stitches were done on my wound and I was screaming madly throughout the surgery. What a harrowing time the other patients in the hospital would have had, I wondered.

'So, Champ, how did it happen?' Dad asked.

'Actually ... eh ... I missed a bouncer,' I said sheepishly.

'Really?'

'Dad, my friends are bad. I won't play with them anymore,' I said and hugged him.

'No dear, don't feel that way, it happens sometimes ... you see sometimes friends go wrong ...'

'No, they are not wrong; I hate them.' I felt a lump in my throat but I didn't cry.

And, that was another end of something that I loved—my Big Boyz gang and our evening play. Dad tried his best to persuade me to go around again but I was stubborn and even Mom opposed him and asked Dad not to force me. My world contracted inside the four walls of my room after school. Sometimes, Shalini would visit but most of the days I remained alone watching the endless *saas bahu* sagas with Mom. You see, they really improve your patience.

'Mom, these serials suck ... I mean how could you watch them even,' I exclaimed.

'What did you say?' She was surprised to hear the word "suck" from me. 'From where did you learn such words?'

'Oh my God! This boy is going out of hand day by day,' she bawled.

'What happened? I don't understand. See, the other day, I and Shalini were watching a movie in HBO and I heard the word there. I guess this word is used to show frustration,' I clarified.

'What ...? You watch English movies too?'
'Yeah! What's the big deal?'

An end again ... and this time Mom made sure that I don't watch English films.

∽

I was admitted to a music school to learn Guitar, so that I could utilise my time doing something fruitful rather than getting involved in something which was considered 'not good' by my Mom for a boy of eleven.

It was altogether a new experience for me. I had never been attracted to music ever in my life before entering the doors of Danny's Musical. Danny—cool name, I thought. And believe me, the man himself was as cool as his name. At six feet, he was a fair and sturdy middle-aged man with long hair! He had pierced half-a-dozen of rings on his left ear and wore sleeveless shirts/t-shirts most of the time to show off his big tattoo on his equally spread biceps.

My Mom did raise her eyebrows over his funky looks but then it was her decision that music would do good to me and she possibly couldn't backtrack after brainwashing me so much. She had contemplated other options as well, like:

- Karate ... but then she thought ... *no violence for my son ...!*
- Dance ... there was a rumour spread; *the masterji there molested kids ... out of question.*
- Cricket ... Mom didn't like the game. And moreover, she didn't want me to go back to my 'ill-mannered' friends.
- Swimming ... there were no separate batches for girls and boys. *A strict no-no ... thought my Mom.*

Moreover, there were other good reasons in favour of the Guitar class. Girls don't get attracted to guitar and that's why, rarely one finds any girl joining classes to learn. So, no doubt at all, I was put in to learn guitar.

On my very first day there, I was more nervous than happy to discover the world of music. I sat in an empty hall alone, waiting for the rest of the class to come. I steered my eyes around, to have an idea of the new domain and zeroed on a guitar leaning on the chair. There was something special about that dead stringed instrument which made my soul alive. I deliberately walked towards it and picked it. I plucked the strings and carefully listened to the calm resonance. And then, my eyes fell on the notebook placed on a stand-table.

'What's written in this?' I thought as I scrolled through the pages full of dashes, dots and strange symbols.

'Don't worry son, you would be able to understand them very soon,' it was Danny, standing behind me.

We were ten in our batch, all of the same age but not all were beginners. Most of them knew how to read the chords and also were trying their hand on the strings. From my side, I didn't even know how to hold it but then that's what Danny needed. Danny believed it's easier to teach someone who knows nothing rather the one who knew something.

'So, before I start, I want you to delete everything from your mind, whatever you know about music. Just follow what I am saying,' Danny announced from the dais.

'Okay sir,' we all roared.

'No "sir". Call me Danny.'

First, he gave us a brief introduction of guitar with a demonstration on all the parts of the guitar which somewhat reminded me of our biology class in school wherein the boys excitedly looked on and girls giggled under as our teacher went through the details about the whole human body system.

Danny then showed us the right way to hold the guitar. And, the next order was to do whatever we wished for the next ten minutes. I know strumming madly is something weird but we were all enjoying, especially we beginners. We had a few more of such exercises which helped us to have a feel of the instrument.

As expected, Mom came to pick me up after the class. As we walked the way home, she asked me about the class. I smiled at her and said: 'Mom, thanks for bringing me here. I am loving it.'

I *still* remember

'So Danny, what do you think?' I asked anxiously as he completed reading my song.

'Cool! Boy,' Danny exclaimed. 'So, ... are you going to sing it in your farewell party ... (I nodded) to impress your girl?'

'My girl!' What a joke, I thought. Was my song really for a girl or was Danny just trying to boost my morale by saying this to kill my stage fright?

'Girl? Who?'

'Yeah, that tall one,' he said.

'Who ... Shalini? Oh! Come on, you must be crazy to think like that.'

'Oh! Please, don't mind. Just that everybody talks about you two a lot; which is why I thought.'

'She is just a very good friend of mine and anyway, I am just sixteen,' I defended.

'Sixteen ... so what? There is no age bar for love,' he said as a matter of fact. I smiled as some old memories of Shamita flashed before me. I wanted to tell Danny about her ... but decided not to.

'Anyway, she is taller than me,' I said and finally he stopped talking on that any further.

'Danny, crap the bloody topic. Just tell me, will you please compose the music for me?'

'Sure, but I want you to try yourself first,' Danny said with a tap on my back.

'You must be crazy, Danny.'

'C'mon, don't put my name down. It's been four years you're learning guitar.'

Four years! Wow! My romance with the six-strings had really been a long-time affair and I never seemed to have noticed the pace of time that went by. So, in that case, I thought why not give it a shot ... its's not that big a deal to compose the tune. Heart of heart I knew I could and I did.

'Danny, how is this now?' I said after playing the tune, I had composed.

'It's wonderful, but I suggest that you should increase the note a bit more,' he advised.

'Like this?' I said as I pressed *b-string* instead of *g-string*.

'Yeah, now go ahead with the song.'

I smiled back at him as I moved my fingers quick along the strings and went on with my first composition ...

I still remember the tears rolling down,
Everything coming to an abrupt end;
The feeling of insecurity
Torture and aloofness.
Standing at the casement
And watching her go ...

34 Mom says no Girlfriend

The memories are hazy but feelings are pure,
I'll miss you P.R.I.A, I'll miss you for sure...

I still remember my achievements in school,
Full marks in maths,
My trophy for debate,
Running all over the hurdles
Cheering my house for a goal...
The strings spreading music in the air,
My futile efforts to paint
And the brushes full of colours
Each day my hard washed uniforms
Would be stained with my childish strokes,
And above all, mom would stare in the eye ...
I still remember my friend
My wit and sense for me
The one who held my hand
When no one pitied on me,
My philosopher, my guide,
A hard face out,
But soft from inside
She was one with the difference
My teacher and preacher as well,
Looking, caring and treating me,
Like her own child.

I will never forget the memories
Worth a fortune for me
And today as I say adieu to my school
I raise my hands in prayer and say
Return me the day once more

I still remember 35

The first day of my school
The way I clenched mom's hands
The way dad left me in my class
Let me again feel the pang of sticks
Let me again stand in front of my class to mind
With pleasure I would shed my youth
If I get my childhood days back in full.
My childhood and my innocence
Again to cherish the reminiscence
The memories go hazy but feelings remain pure
I'll miss you P.R.I.A, I'll miss you for sure ...

'Howazzat?' I cried out in Danny's *ishtyle* after I finished the song.

'Boy, I am proud of you,' he said and embraced me. 'The song will rock, you see to it.'

And it really did. Though I was very much apprehensive standing on the stage, I knew that it was my last chance to be on the hall of fame. For this was something the least expected from a boy who always feared to even read a chapter in class; singing in front of two hundred odd people was no less than an experience of walking on the moon. I had a look at the audience before I started my Herculean act. Each and every pair of eyes was stuck on me, my heart which was already beating fast accelerated even more. But then, as I hit the chords with the pluck turm, the euphony soothed my mind and I lost to my own world of harmony. There was a strange silence as I went on ahead with my song. But finally, the atmosphere changed when I went up with the scales and my friends joined me in chorus. Needless to say, I was the star of the evening.

'So Samarth, what are you planning to study further,' Nair Ma'am asked me.

'I don't know Ma'am, I have not yet thought of it ... may be music.' I answered.

'Now that's something really different from the line. Make sure your parents allow you,' Ma'am replied and I wondered why my parents will not allow, after all they were the ones who made me join the guitar class.

At home ... the scene was not something I expected ...

'Somu, have you gone crazy? We have already planned everything. You're going to be an Engineer and hence study science,' Mom bawled at me. 'There's a boom of engineering in the world and don't forget there are so many hopes pinned on you.'

'I don't care what the rest of the world is thinking; it's my life after all,' I rebelled.

'See, we sent you for the guitar classes so that there is some mood change for you apart from just studies. You expressed your desire to continue learning for four more years and we allowed. But now it's enough, and you should do something meaningful now. It's time to give your life a shape.'

'What? What do you mean by mood change? It was you, who had forced me to join the guitar classes,' I snivelled. 'It was you who took me there and now you only want me to end it.'

'Somu, we are your parents. We know what's good and bad for you, you're not old enough to take your own decisions,' Mom declared. I knew there was no point in arguing, my fate was already written and couldn't be changed, so I gave in.

'What happened, Champ?' Danny inquired. 'What is it that's eating you? Tell me, maybe I can help you.'

'The college is starting from tomorrow which means this is the last day of mine here,' I whined.

'You're upset for such a silly reason? C'mon, you're grown up now, don't behave like a child.'

'You very well know how much I love guitar.'

'I understand you and also your parents, they are not wrong either ... And who told you this is your last day here? We will meet every Sunday. Don't worry; I will make sure that you don't miss anything.'

'Really?' I asked out of joy and gave him a tight hug.

'Sam, your Dad loves you very much.'

'I know that,' I said. It was clear that it had to be Dad who mooted the idea of Sunday classes.

ॐ

Unlike my friends, I was really not happy with my college because of the schedule. I had to wake up at 5.00 a.m. everyday and that was not all. To reach there was another nightmare. Anybody could easily earn an A grade in NCC; the trip to college was that strenuous!

After waking up at 5 a.m. it was a mad mad rush for me to be able to catch the 6.10 a.m. bus. This mad rush and the run every morning to the bus stand helped me in winning the two km marathon race in the annual sport meet of my college!

Rasayani (my home town) didn't have a college during my time. So boarding the first bus to Panvel was itself no less than a MTV *Roadies* task. But then that was not all, once you're down from the almost *death ride*, the destination remained still far away.

My college was one and a half km away (through shortcut) from the bus stand. The shortcut was dirty, dangerous and dodgy. The road was old and broken with tall bushes on both sides; reckoning the slum's closeness I and the other students who used the shortcut preferred walking on the narrow road in spite of the risk of getting run over by a vehicle. Next, we had to balance ourselves on the stone to avoid falling in the open drain created by the municipality. Finally, after crossing the highway and trotting a couple of streets and climbing over a wall, we reached the playground of C.K.T. Jr. College! I guess all the students of the college deserved a *Padmashree* more than Saif Ali Khan for being made to undergo such torture and still reporting to class on time!

It was compulsory to maintain an attendance of 85 percent, else one was not allowed to sit for the exams. We had four teachers each for every subject, so at a time four chapters per subject were on and the four back-to-back classes ensured that there was no way we could get some time off in between the periods. Moreover, the class test every week denied us any social life. So, life in C.K.T. was all about learning and studying with an aim to make students ready for IITs and AIIMs. But the memories there haunt one's mind so much that hardly anyone is able to perform well at the entrance exams! Yet, in spite of all the strictness and not to forget the ardous journey, there is a mad rush of students for admission every year. I guess it's the cool name C.K.T. which attracts.

I was the only one from Rasayani in my class. Quite disheartened of this fact, I entered Room No: 111 at the ground floor. Without the nostalgic excitement to be among the back benchers and enjoying the college life with my group of friends, I opted to choose the first benches.

'Hello,' I said to the guy sitting next to me. He too seemed to be in the same situation like me—no friends, and he smiled back. It was the Chemistry lecture and I was a bit late for the class. Being the first day, I was not scolded, yet the teacher's expression meant that I should be careful next time.

'Whose period ... (I bit my tongue, I had to remind myself that it's no longer school, we are in college, so I quickly corrected myself) I mean ... which lecture is next?'

'It's Patil sir's lecture.'

'I guess this one was Patil sir's lecture.'

'Yeah, you're right but unfortunately the next one too is of Patil sir.'

'Okay, so two consecutive lectures,' I raised my doubt.

'Not really, the names of both professors are the same.'

'Really?'

'Don't make faces; you would be surprised to know that all teachers are Patils,' he said in delight.

'I know it creates confusion so I've drawn their cartoons to remember beneath their names,' he showed me the time-table.

'That's good but I think remembering them by their first name may also help, or are they same too,' I suggested.

'Eh... no, thank God ...! It's a good idea. You're smart,' he seemed to be amazed by my answer which was only logical.

'Well, ... I am Samarth Sinha,' I introduced. 'What about you?'

'I am Amar Patil.'

I thought of not getting on further with him and looked around to avoid him; to my surprise the class had almost gone empty for the next lecture, the reason was, of course, the subject being the most boring—Physics.

'I think even we must leave,' Amar said to me.

'What about the attendance?' I asked; the 85 percent theory still haunting my mind.

'It's just one lecture and anyway we can bunk one lecture every day still our attendance will be well above the target,' he came up with a detailed calculation on the same in his notebook.

I was literally fed up of his analysis and to avoid him I just ran outside. But he was following me like my shadow.

'See, it's not worth wandering around like this,' he said.

'Then let's go somewhere, maybe to the canteen,' I suggested and he agreed.

My school never had a canteen and I always missed it. I mean, I've seen all those canteen scenes like the chats, fights, proposals and all in movies and TV serials and was feeling very happy about the fact that my college had one. But then it was nowhere around my expectation. It was just like a normal *tapri* type, only one man standing, cooking and serving, no table, no chairs ... a shabby joint! So, I never bothered to check the menu either due to disappointment. And moreover, the English medium, semi-English medium and Marathi medium all had the recess at the same time, and getting something from the canteen was no wonder, a mammoth task, still my *not yet friend* took a chance and plunged in.

Fifteen minutes later finally, I could see a guy with distorted clothes, messy hair and fluttering tie struggling to come outside the sea of humanity. I gave my hand and pulled him outside.

'Thanks,' he said.

'My pleasure,' I acknowledged.

'Actually, I had just five rupees with me so I could get only one *vada-paav*,' he said. 'But we can share it ... so this one is for our friendship.'

I was not at all interested in eating the *vada-paav* but still appreciating his gesture I agreed and we sat on the wall which separated our college ground and the CIDCO Park, enjoying half *vada-paav* each.

'Are you from this school?' I asked.

'Yeah! And you?'

'I am from P.R.I.A.'

'What? That's a funny name,' he mocked.

'Well ... it stands for Patalganga Rasayani Industrial Association.' I cleared his doubt. I loved my school and hated such remarks.

'Okay, I got it,' he said rather sheepishly and we stayed silent for few seconds before he initiated again.

I am sorry ... friends?' He said and brought his hands forward.

They say, the first impression is the last impression but it does not go right with Amar. I have always been a shy guy and hate getting into a situation wherein everybody is looking at me. And with Amar, life was full of embarrassments. For the next few days in C.K.T. he was my only friend. He always had his own analysis and calculation on everything around and I never doubted him, just followed him. Moreover, I loved being with him because he was clean from the heart and is still the same person.

Meeting Mr Legend

'Now that's not fair, it's not even been a month and they announced the dates for the first unit test,' I bawled in disgust.

'And what about the journals, how are we going to complete them?' Amar echoed my voice further but nobody seemed to be interested since there was no point in crying or arguing. The datesheet was already pinned on the notice board!

Following Amar's *one-class-bunk* theory, we sat at the adjacent CIDCO Park completing our journals. While we got intuited in drawing strange figures which our Patil Ma'am says are all inside our body, the people around were happy to see that the generation next is marching in the right direction. They were oblivious of the fact that great men like us never work seriously until and unless our ass is on fire, literally!

Half an hour later, we realised that it was not possible to finish pending assignments in one hour and two hours later, our fingers gave up and made us realise that it was not possible anymore. We took a break and had a look around the park. In C.K.T. that was my best time-pass, I enjoyed watching activities of people in the park and I did it even from my class which had its windows facing the park. In the morning, it were the elderly who would come to jog, debate or to do yoga; the noon shift was reserved to people madly in love, while in the evening children gathered around to play.

Of all the unknown faces around, my eyes finally stuck on a familiar face. I reckoned, I had seen him rarely but heard of him plenty in class. He was Amey Pandit, the popular playboy of our college. Legend behind him revealed that he could make any damn woman sleep with him. He himself claimed to have lost his virginity while in the seventh class. I was very curious about him and didn't want to miss an opportunity to meet him. So, I approached him.

'Hi!' I greeted but he didn't look at me at all, instead he was busy adjusting the antenna of his walky phone.

'Hi, I am Samarth. I am in your class.' I introduced and this time he did turn to look at me but rather angrily. I thought my timing was wrong and drew my steps back.

'Hey, you geek! Just come here,' he screamed at me and handed me the copper wire attached to the antenna. 'Stretch your hands up holding this wire ... and don't try to listen to what I am talking.'

Though he spoke very low, I could make out that he was speaking to a girl, other than that I didn't try to listen or observe. Actually, I was so scared of his aggression that I didn't even dare to gaze at him.

'Thank you,' he said quite generously after he ended the call.

'Please, mention not, it's okay, we are classmates after all.'

'Really?' he said, I don't know whether it was a question or a statement.

'You're right, champ ... girls are indeed evil,' he patted my back and left.

I was really astounded because that was the third time somebody had said that to me. I returned to Amar, he was like quite delighted to have solved some equation on his notepad. Curiosity getting the better of me, I peeped inside his notepad to know what held his interest so much:

$$\text{Girls} = \text{time} \times \text{money}$$
$$\text{Time} = \text{money}$$
$$\therefore \text{Girls} = \text{money} \times \text{money}$$
$$\text{Girls} = (\text{money})^2$$
$$\text{Money} = \sqrt{\text{evil}} \text{ (because money is the root cause of all evil)}$$
$$\therefore \text{Girls} = (\sqrt{\text{evil}})^2$$
$$\text{Girls} = \text{evil}$$

Oh, no! Not again ... I thought.
'What's this?' I asked out of frustration.
'What?'
'The damn equation that you have there,' I replied.
'Oh! Well, I didn't create it ... it's ... it's printed on your t-shirt, buddy,' Amar replied rather cheekily.
'Whaaaat?' I said in surprise and looked down on my t-shirt; Amar was right.
'Man, you don't have to pretend that you don't know about it?' he said.
'No, I am not pretending ... actually Mom bought it yesterday only. I didn't check it out.'
'That's something weird now; you get just one day in a week to come in civil dress and your Mom selects what you should wear then too,' Amar said with such an expression as if I were an alien. I don't like such comments but it was true, it's a weird thing and I chose not to speak about it. Amar could guess that I didn't like his comment.

'Sorry,' he paused after the apology only to reiterate his *friends na* hand-shake for the fifth time that day! It only irritated me even more.

∾

I knew it won't pass through my throat yet, I gave it a try considering the fact that I might not be able to write the three hour's chemistry paper empty stomach. It was again Amar who dared to bring it. The '*it*' was the *missal-paav,* a mixed curry of *matar*, *chana* and some more from the same family with stale buns or *paav*.

'What's this?' I asked Amar, picking up a soft, red, cylindrical thing.

'It's *rajma*,' he replied matter of fact.

'Oh! Rajma ... I never knew rajma had got legs! I said rather sarcastically.

'God damn! These are not legs, you fool ... these are its sprouts,' he said out of frustration. 'Give it to me, I'll eat it,' and he picked it from my hand and put it in his mouth. I heard a crunch as Amar chewed.

Amar's expression changed. He looked at me and said: 'Do you think it was a cockroach?'

'Yes, Amar ... a baby cockroach.' My answer was enough to make him go nuts, vomiting and rinsing his mouth repeatedly at the washbasin.

I was not sure of the equations on the chemistry paper but yes, there was a definite chemical imbalance in my stomach and the reaction inside was even worse. People around me had already experienced it but were not sure, who the culprit really was. I was going all restless just looking around and doing nothing which was enough to attract the invigilator.

'Show me your pockets,' ordered the invigilator. I stood up and he checked me up and down but was disappointed. However, he was not of that kind to let it go that easy, he kept a constant watch on me. He was confident that Amey won't let him down and his hunch was right. As the invigilator stood beside him, his expression was all similar to the one Jerry (of Tom and Jerry) has when caught eating cheese by Tom. But I guess teachers in C.K.T. are far more ferocious than Tom.

My condition was more miserable than Amey's as the volcano inside had almost reached my mouth and I felt pukish. With one hand on my stomach caressing the cramps and one on my mouth, I tried my very best to control but then one sight of a diagram of a cockroach in the girl next's paper reminded me everything and the volcano erupted and … the whole arthropod soup was on my paper. I had everything sucrose, fructose and glucose on my paper, yet I got a zero in the paper!

∽

It's not every day, you encounter a live smooch scene at the garden but I was not interested at all. I knew Mom would kill me for getting a zero and so I decided to spend some time in the park. Amar tried his best to make me feel better but nothing could move me. I chose to remain quiet and kept looking down at the ground.

'Come on, it was not your fault,' Amar said for the seventh straight time and I returned him my most dirty look. He understood and stayed silent for a moment.

'Friends,' he said extending his hands towards me.

'Fuck off you idiot, don't dare do that again,' I shouted at him and tapped back his hands which were unlikely hard. It was definitely not him and I looked up. To my surprise it was Mr Legend, and Amar was nowhere near me!

'Eh ... sorry, I thought ...' I said, completely taken aback by his presence.

'Don't worry; they will take a re-test of yours later.'

'Really?' I cheered and he nodded. 'Thank you for the news.'

No ... no ... don't thank me ... I should thank you ... ,' he said and I raised an eyebrow.

'See, I had these chits with me and was going to be caught ... when thanks to you the whole class got distracted. You know what I mean, the invigilator drifted towards you and I got time to dispose the chits,' he explained. 'So ... thank you.'

We shook hands and the three of us; Amar also joined; sat to have a chat. Both, me and Amar were amazed listening to his adventure stories and Amey seemed more than happy to narrate them. And finally when his neverending adventure stories ended, Amey offered a small celebration from his side.

'There is a three-day break coming. We will celebrate then,' he suggested. Although I and Amar were reluctant we agreed.

'Anyway, where are we going?' I asked.

'To Taj.'

'What?? No way, they would throw us out. Damn, we are in uniforms,' I protested.

'They won't. Believe me,' he smiled.

And they really didn't, because we were the only ones dressed neatly, the rest wore *lungis* ... Yeah! Guessed it right, Taj was the *dhaba* on the old highway and was remotely even, not anywhere to what I had expected. That was the first time, I was eating at a *dhaba*. Such places are never preferred for good family guys like us, there are obvious reasons of course, hygienically it's said you could always feel the aroma of the dish served earlier on the same plate before you. Never expect etiquettes from the staff (they don't think customer is always right). Whoever you are or from wherever you come, there is no alternative to cozy but tough cots or better say *khatiyas* here in the dhaba.

Barring the atmosphere and the look of the dhaba, the food served was excellent. 'I never have had such delicious butter chicken; thank you Amey for bringing us here,' I said.

'My pleasure dear, I owed you the treat,' Amey said. 'Be comfortable Amar, put your legs up.'

'So, what's so cool here?' Amar asked as he comforted himself on the *khatiya*.

'What do you mean by that?'

'Well, I guess it's cheap, so we are here, right?' Amar initiated his usual interrogation.

'Yeah! That's one of the factors, there is no meaning spending on guys like you.' He paused to look at our expression. 'Just kidding, chill *yaar*. You see, sometimes I like bringing changes in my life and I love being adventurous and wild.'

'What is so wild in this?' I interrupted.

'I don't know what you people expect from me or do I know it very well. C'mon, I thought you people to be good.'

'Hey! We're good or bad ... well ... how much do you know about us? But we know for sure that you're bad?'

'Thank you for the compliment,' Amey bowed. 'Only for Samarth ... tell me, are you a virgin?'

'Why is that question not relevant for me,' Amar protested.

'You know it better than me,' Amey replied. 'Samarth, answer my question.'

I thought for a few seconds and nodded. He just smiled on it.

'Now, this one goes for Amar. Have you ever talked to an opposite sex?' I don't know what really Amey wanted to convey by not using *girls*. Anyway, both of us waited for Amar to answer while he boot scanned his brain to locate a related file but we knew it didn't exist and finally ...

'I am quite sure Amar, you might not have seen a porn flick either,' Amey escaped the process and Amar shook his head instantly.

'You're a bloody jerk,' Amey declared.

'What's the big deal in that, even I've not seen any,' I regretted my spontaneous reaction seeing Amey's expression. 'Well ... not exactly porn, but I do watch the late night shows on AXN,' Amey still seemed to be highly disappointed.

'Hey! I had once seen that movie—*The Girl Next Door*. It's about a porn star and so you can say that I do have a bit of idea about them. Elisha Cuthbert looks awesome, I just love her. She is my favourite,' I replied trying to save the situation for myself.

'Hey! I know her, too. She comes in Popular Mechanics for Kids in the Discovery channel.'

'Really? Did you know that she almost stripped in the movie and the kisses were just fabulous.'

'I want to watch it too ... please,' Amar howled but it hadn't impressed Amey at all.

'You both are sick. Go and sit on your mother's lap,' he bawled at us. The last line reminded me of something which I hate most ... *Mamma's Boy* ... not again, I thought. Somewhere I felt, he was right. Teens are the best days of one's life, full of fun and new adventures and experiences; however, we were yet to experience that.

After the treat, Amey drove us to a pub- Krazy Boyz. It was closed though.

'Why the hell did you stop here?' I asked.

'Look at that pub,' Amey pointed at the pub.

'Okay ... so what's so special about that pub?'

'It's heaven; I will take you there one day.'

'Oh! Really, will you?'

'But for that, you need to prove yourself.'

'Like ... how?' Amar questioned.

'Watch a porn flick first and I will decide after that,' Amey replied with a slick smile.

My first sex

'Hello,' I said.

It was our neighbour in whom's house we went to receive phone calls. We didn't have a phone at that time.

'Eureka! I got it,' Amar cried through the phone, loud enough to be audible to Aunty.

'Take it easy, man,' I said to Amar, looking sheepishly at Aunty.

'I got the B.P.,' he shouted again, this time a few decibels higher. There was no use begging Amar, nothing could deter his spirits. So, I thought disconnecting the line was a better idea. Aunty was still peering at me, suspiciously.

'Actually, I had asked my friend for a *Bhajan Puja* CD and it seems he got it,' I explained.

'Really?' she narrowed her eyes. 'I know really well what kind of *bhajans* you guys see,' she said with a very cunning smile as I left.

'Enjoy it,' she shouted at my back.

Next day, we bunked the rest of the class after the recess for the big show ahead. It was Thursday and Amar's Mom usually visits a nearly temple. So, we had nearly two hours of free viewing with us and, Amar had struck on a jackpot.

'Your brother has got a damn big collection. How did you know about it?'

'I was suspecting him for a long time. I don't think he studied that hard every night, how come he got those A.T.K.Ts then. I had searched my PC many times but never found anything,' he paused to show me a key.

'It's his cupboard's key ... I stole this from his bag and see where I've landed on—a porn treasure!!!!!' Amey said excitedly and with the same emotion he inserted the CD in the tray.

The feeling was all different; neither had I experienced that before nor ever after that. So, describing those moments now is very much difficult. All I can say, that our excitement was taken over by astonishment in a few seconds after the video went on. We were aghast and our hearts were thumping fast as never before.

'Do you think they are real?' Amar asked.

'Real? What do you mean?'

'I mean ... eh ... it's dirty. Does everybody do it this way; I think you are not understanding what I am trying to say,' he said. I very well understood what Amar meant but didn't want to think about it at all and excused myself from it.

'How do I know, Amar? Better ask Amey, he knows it well.'

We had won our challenge; we had crossed our first hurdle to heaven. It was time to meet Amey and take our prize; we called at his home number from a booth in the park. His phone was one of the first to have ringtones and I loved hearing the songs he set as ringtones. But then ... I paused ... how was I able to hear his ringtone so clearly ? To my surprise Amey was standing right behind me.

'Why do you carry your phone always?' I inquired.

'Well,' he smiled, 'I had asked my Dad for a cell, he refused and so I am using this landphone till he buys me one. You see, I have so many calls to attend. Anyways how was it watching the stuff you had never seen?'

'It was good, everything quite different in real when compared to Mr Patil's diagrams on the board,' I joked.

'Watch a few more of them and your Chapter 18 is complete.'

'And what about that girl-girl thing, they were kissing each other so passionately. How could they do so? Have they gone nuts? Why not have men fuck them?'

'See, they're lesbians. If the same exists amongst men then it's called gay. It's very strange you don't know about it. It's really very common in the West; here too it's getting popular,' Amey patiently cleared all our doubts in detail. But we were not at all interested, perhaps were more edgy to know what next to get into the pub.

'Amey, c'mon, it's enough now. I can't wait anymore, please tell us about Krazy Boyz,' cried a rather baffled Amar.

'I told you the place is heaven.'

'Yeah! We know that. Tell us something that we don't know.'

'See, it's not that easy getting into heaven, you've to sacrifice first.'

'Sacrifice ... as in?'

'Well, your good boys image will go for a toss then. I mean, you just have one life ... so one should enjoy it to the fullest ... smoke, drink, fuck ...'

'What???' I screamed.

Life with Amey was like jaunting in the space. Doesn't matter from where you begin, you always have an infinite path on all the four sides. You kind of get lost and you never want to come back again. He believes, there is nothing that is good or bad but the thinking that makes it so and we all had good thoughts regarding smoking, so we were trying it.

'C'mon, go ahead,' Amey insisted. I was though a bit apprehensive to kiss the butt of the cigarette. I looked at Amar who had already had half of it in his mouth. With a few more coughs and a fair bit of struggle, the flame reached the filter finally. However, I couldn't. The smell of burning tobacco was stinking and it sort of clogged my brain and literally burnt my chest, I hate them.

'I can't do it,' I surrendered. 'Maybe, I can score in drink.'

'No, you won't be able to, I bet,' Amey hailed at me.

It was drinks next and we needed a venue for it as it was not possible in the park. A night out was the need of the occasion and that was something impossible for me. However, with the help of Amey, finally Dad permitted for combined studies ... what else could one say! So, the party was at Amey's place as his parents were out to their native place. We had beer to start with along with chicken lollipop and chips as *chakna*.

'Condition is that only one goes with me to the Pub. Amar is clearly leading, so Sam, you will have to try harder. One bottle extra than Amar,' Amey announced.

Looking at the size of the bottle, I thought it was not a big deal; I had finished a two litre bottle of Coke during Diwali at the society competition, so this seemed relatively easy for me. I was confident I would win here too. Amey poured beer in the glasses; it exhibited urine-like colour and the smell was even more offensive. I didn't comment anything there. We put our glasses together for *Cheers*. I took a sip and drew it away. Both of them looked blank at me. I sulked some of it in and my face shrunk at the centre, the cough syrup tasted better, I thought.

'I don't know why people pay so much for this. It tastes awful,' I said as I finished my glass.

'Man! It would be bitter for beginners like you,' Amey explained. 'Stuff some *chakna*, it will be easy then to drink.'

'Don't understand why people are so crazy about it. I mean what is it worth, really? I hate it, I will never drink again. Hell, with your pub, I want my money back.' Even I didn't have an idea, why I was speaking all that. I reckoned the beer had already started to show its effect with just two glasses in.

'Sam, you're already among the stars. Don't forget you had to beat Amar.'

I looked at Amar; he was all calm and composed sipping through glasses after glasses. Since past few days, he had stopped using his super brain much and had been marching slowly and steadily to each and every winning post. I couldn't let this dumbo win again, I thought. He finally ended with two bottles and I searched for *chakna* as I picked my third bottle.

'Sorry, we've ran out of *chakna*,' Amey said. I knew it was going to be difficult without it but was not ready to lose. I picked the bottle in one hand and blocked my nose with the other hand; I finished the bottle in just one breath. Something which always worked when I had to consume those medicines in my childhood.

'Bravo!' cheered Amey and I rushed to the bathroom to empty my stomach ... from my mouth!

༄

Life was like never before, finally I had options beyond Danny's music classes. The one-class-bunk theory was history as we had found new ways to maintain our attendance. We became more regular at the Rupali Cinema's morning shows than Patil Sir's labs. I learnt to lie to Mom, beg to my cousins and steal (sometimes) from Dad for my expenses. Except Sunday's musical classes, I never felt like returning to Rasayani.

'Hey Sam, what's up?' it was Shalini after a long time.

'Nothing really, had gone to Danny,' I answered.

'I know that. But how come you are rarely seen here these days.'

'C.K.T. rocks, I told you too to take admission here but you went to J.H. Ambani.'

'Sam, you've gone mad. A new life, new friends, girls, adventures, smoking, drinking, right?' She said in a way I didn't understand, was she disappointed or happy for me. From my side, I stayed mum. I couldn't lie to her.

'Like all other guys, you've become bad, too,' she said with a smile and left.

In the months to come, we had few more of combined studies sessions whenever Amey's parents were out. We experimented on qualities and quantities alternatively on whatever we tried. By the second semester of twelfth, Amar was already a chain smoker; I was a complete *bewda* while Amey became the all-rounder. And then came the big day or should I say the big night.

'So guys, are you nervous,' Amey asked, as we stood outside Krazy Boyz.

'Amey, are you sure that we're ready for it ... I mean ... we are just seventeen, let's wait till we are eighteen at least,' I suggested.

'Fuck off Sam; I've waited for this since long. Don't worry I got full setting in. This is my third time here. Don't worry, it would be safe,' he explained. Amar nodded too with Amey perhaps, he was the one most excited. He had this quote written on his T– '*do you believe in love at first sight or should I pass again*'.

'Now what's that? And, why are you wearing pink.' I exclaimed.

'Girls love pink.'

'Yeah! True but I don't know why? What do you think, Amey?'

'What? You don't know the reason, watch the porn movies carefully you would understand,' he said. I still didn't get it though.

'C'mon, hell with it let's get in,' Amey and Amar pushed me in.

I don't think it was Amey's third visit. He was quite popular there, most of the people there knew him. We made our way to one of the corners in the pub. The music was on an ear splitting note yet nobody was complaining, they were just grooving along with their partners on the dance floor on the popular item numbers. Amar and I sat on a cozy sofa while Amey went to see someone. Couple of minutes later, Amey returned to call us.

'I think we should try this too *yaar*. It looks fun,' Amar cried looking at a pale guy who was sniffing some white powder with a rolled paper.

'Amar, that's drugs ... even I've not gone to that level,' Amey replied.

He took us to another room where three girls were waiting, I guessed, for us. There were three facts I was completely sure about, first, they were older than us, secondly we were born lucky and lastly, the night was going to be very long and wild. They all cheered up seeing us but we (me and Amar, of course) were shy and just returned blank smiles.

'Cool, t-shirt boy. And it's pink, I love it,' one of them teased Amar. Wow! It worked, kudos to Amar and his analysis.

'Boys, meet Sophie, Shefali and Nutan. And girls, this is Sam and this is Amar,' Amey introduced us. All the three girls took a better look at us before they got involved in some discussion. Five minutes later, it was declared who was to sleep ... oops ... I mean who was to go with whom—Sophie-Amar, Shefali-Amey and Nutan-Sam. The venue was of course ... Amey's home.

'This is not done, Amey,' I grumbled.

'C'mon, we will swap partners later.'

'No, you idiot, I'm not talking about that. Don't you think it's going to be awkward? I mean sex is okay ... but not together. How can I go naked in front of you and Amar?'

'Asshole! Won't you mind stripping before the girls? Anyway, that's what group sex is. Don't worry; you won't realise your own presence during the act, sex rocks ... believe me!'

'But you've your whole house empty, *na*?'

'So what, I cannot use my parent's and sister's room for these things. We will take on different corners, *yaar*. Take it easy, what is really troubling you, it's okay between friends. Be a bit practical. Look at Amar, he is already enjoying each moment of it.'

I gazed at him, the 'all-time geek' was in real heaven. All the three ladies had surrounded him as he completely relaxed on the sofa with hands and legs spread. Amar stood up to remove his T but they pulled him back.

'Don't, your T is cool,' remarked one of them.

'Funny', I thought.

Ten minutes on, the girls were still with Amar and ... except his T everything else on the floor!! Amar seemed completely hypnotised by the feeling; he seemed to be altogether in some other world.

'Girls, we are here, too,' Amey screamed.

Reluctantly though, two of them walked towards us ... we paired and went to the opposite corners.

'What's your name?' I asked her.

'Setuka,' she replied instantly.

'But I guess ... Amey said you were Nutan at the pub.'

'Then why are you asking, dumbo? Why do you want to know my name? Want to tell your Momma about me?' she laughed and the other girls chimed in, too.

'You're a virgin, right? (I nodded) I love being fucked by virgins. You guys give the full control,' she rejoiced.

I kept standing and waited for her to initiate. She was more than happy to take the lead. She was wonderful. I was completely flown away by the feeling. All I remember is the wonderful ... wonderful ... feeling which I will never be able to forget all my life.

Suddenly, I remembered about Amey's advice; I tore a condom packet but was, however, confused not knowing how to use it. She guessed from my expression and helped me out.

'What do you do?' I asked, struggling.

'Kid, you're a dork. Stop your nonsense and put on some real efforts.'

ϖ

I looked at the wall clock, it was four. I was awake yet kept my eyes shut as I lay at one side of the bed completely tired. We had sex twice and she was initiating for the third time. I pretended to be asleep. Amey and Amar were still batting in their second innings after swapping their partners, while my partner cursed and abused me avidly. But I pretended to be asleep, she gave up and went for a few more drinks before she also finally tumbled down. I too dozed off soon.

'Wake up. Wake up, you jerk,' Amey kicked. My head was spinning, as I woke up. It was quite bright around. 'Your Mom is on the line.'

'Nothing Mom ... I was studying late ... yeah! Would come back soon,' I said and hung up the phone.

Staying away

'Somu, you've a call,' Mom called.

I knew it was from Amey; that was his fifth call of the day, yet I didn't want to talk to him. I don't know why, but I was depressed losing my virginity the other night and was mourning since then. I just shut myself off completely from everything and kept regretting! My behaviour was a bit concerning for Mom and she kept hovering around me asking me if everything was okay, and I knew if she continued doing that I would just breakdown and confess. So, to avoid further suspicion, I went to talk to Amey.

'Hello,' I said.

'Sam, where are you? What happened *yaar*? Is everything okay with you? Why are you not coming to college? And ... for God sake will you utter a word now?' Amey was sounding worried.

'Amey ... allow me to speak, buddy.'

'Okay sorry ... now shoot,' he shouted.

'We will talk tomorrow. I will come to college,' I hung up.

I was shocked to see Aunty standing behind me, putting an ear to our conversion. I looked at her in a way like I never did before. I knew her since two years when she had got married and came to this house and had been quite regular at her place but never ever did I notice her long hair which extended till her waist. She was a beautiful woman in her late twenties; I looked down as I realised that.

'Everything alright?' she inquired.

'Yeah!' I ran away to my room and locked myself again.

I was not sure what was it actually, I was feeling completely messed up. That's exactly how I am, not knowing what's going in my mind, Shalini has been my all time troubleshooter. I thought of seeing her but that would screw the situation further. I waited till next morning.

'You're behaving like you had been raped the other night,' Amey cried in disgust.

'Fuck off Amey, you do not understand me. I have all changed after that night. I mean, the way I used to look at women earlier, it's all different now,' I tried to explain.

'What do you mean?'

'I mean I was ogling at my Aunty ... the phone aunty, remember.'

'It seems you're getting attracted towards elderly ladies. But your c/o aunty has a very sweet voice, what's her age?' Amey asked rather curiously.

'May be 28–29, don't know exactly?'

'Hey, that's not too old. The girls, other night were also of 22–23 ... enjoy yourself,' he lauded.

'Fuck you,' I protested.

'I think you need to learn a few more cusses, I am now bored of it. Try something new,' he laughed. 'Anyway, it's normal at this age. Don't worry, just avoid her and ask your Dad to get a phone now to save his son from getting raped again.'

∽

I got the news from Shalini. It was hard to believe ... I rushed to check and she was right. The board was already pulled down; furniture were already on the truck and instruments were being carried, Danny's musical was closing and for ever. I searched for Danny all over and finally found him at the office. I didn't say anything though, but he understood everything.

'I was to come to you after this but it's good though that you are here. You saved a lot of time ... champ,' he said but I was still silent.

'See, I have to go ... my mother isn't keeping well and she needs me. You have learnt all that I had to teach you; there is no need for you to attend any more classes. Don't worry, I will write letters to you and once you grow up, you can work with me.'

'You'd said you will not leave me ever.'

'C'mon, I am not your wife to stay along,' he joked. I narrowed my eyes, furiously.

'Sorry, but I lied,' he said and took out a case from his pocket. I had seen it earlier; it had his first pluck-turm. 'It's all yours now.'

I didn't accept it and ran away from there. I couldn't watch him go. My respect, my devotion, my love for him all dissolved, I hated him. Though I think he was not selfish. I was not even willing to hear anything of him, I argued with Mom for that and left the dinner half-way. And as usual it was Dad who came to console.

'Son, it seems you're depressed. What happened?' he initiated.

'Dad please, not now. Just leave me alone.'

'It's okay but see what Danny gave me for you.'

'I know, throw it outside. It's not mine, I don't want it.'

I was living in a world of dreams and facing the reality was quite apocalyptic. Over the years, I had got habituated to Danny. He was not just my mentor, he was everything to me. He was gone and I was all alone once again. But then I thought, that was not the end; I have new friends and have my own life to lead, I just need to take control of the situation and accept things.

∾

'Shalini see, I solved the whole question bank, two days earlier than you,' I said.

'Cool! Finally, you got serious about studies. I am bored of studying, why don't we try something on your guitar.'

'I think watching TV would be a better idea. See it's seven; the Wild Discovery might be on. Let's check out.'

'No Sam, play the guitar for me, please.'

'No way, Shalini, I don't play guitar any more.'

'What?' She appeared shocked to hear my decision. 'You were so passionate about music, you loved it.'

'I don't love it anymore, I changed my goals.'

Sometime ago, I was keeping no stone unturned to achieve my goal. But now that Danny was not there I went into complete hibernation for a few months to follow. I locked myself in my room with heaps of guides and solution sets. I moved around rarely, only to load or unload myself. Bath was rare too, I saved both time and water. It also helped to keep disturbance away. The exam periods were even worse, I mugged up day-night, sometimes even remained sleepless and finally when the results were out, I was well above my target.

'Hey, Sam, this boy is from your school, do you know him?' Amar asked, clapping at the felicitation programme.

'Yeah, he is Paramjeet and I hate him.'

'Why man? I thought he was cool. He got selected to play in a club. He is the star of our college ... and ... girls love him,' Amar kept on praising and I could not take it any longer; praises of your worst enemy from your best friend's mouth. And I had to intervene.

'You, bloody gay!' I reverted angrily and moved out of the hall. Both Amey and Amar followed me.

'Sorry, I didn't mean it,' Amar apologised. 'Friends!' he drew his hands at me.

'It's okay now, but please, you don't talk about him anymore,' I said 'Where are you all taking admissions?'

'I am going into psychology, see, girls with no brain go there to study human mind. A perfect stream for me. My Dad says only few years remain before we get *sansarik* and *samajik*, so get serious and do something. I truly agree with him and so I'm going to enjoy my youth fully,' Amey expressed his future plans quite excitedly.

'I am going to S.I.E.S., computer engineering. My Dad's Army quota helped. The college is awesome,' Amar too was very excited.

'I don't know yet, Dad says telecom is evergreen, maybe, that would be the place I might land on.'

'Hey, you and engineering? Jokes apart ... you loved music na?'

'So? Does anybody care for that? And anyway what's it going to earn for me? Nothing! I will do what the rest of the world is doing,' I screeched out of frustration.

'Okay, we understand. So, did you approach any college?'

'I will do anything that will keep me out of Rasayani. I want to stay away, far among strangers.'

Both—my parents and I were happy, my parents because I chose Telecom and I, for the college. The college was far from my home. So, it was decided that I had to stay somewhere near my college so as to not waste time commuting. Finally, I was free. Amey owned a flat near my college which was rented to students and hence searching for an accommodation was never a problem. It was quite a big house with a spacious hall and two bedrooms. The hall was empty, in one of the rooms stayed two guys from the South, I reckoned from their looks and accent. They always kept their door and mouth shut. I always had a strong urge to check them out but Amey had warned that they're maniacs.

'Hi, I am Samarth,' I introduced. They were sneaking in secretly with a bag; I was relaxing in the hall and had caught them.

'Hello, I am Pondy and that's Cherry,' one of them responded while the other rushed in.

'What happened to him? Everything okay?' I asked with a doubtful expression.

'You need not worry unnecessarily, it's none of your business,' Pondy responded rudely yet maintained a smile for the fact that Amey was my close friend. From my side I didn't bother, too.

When I read and hear people cursing their own *alma mater*, I really feel lucky because I studied in some rocking institutes which had always gifted me with some wonderful memories and so was my new college. Perhaps, my college was beyond my expectations, I realised as I explored the campus on the very first day of my college. Needless to say the college building was an architectural marvel. But the main attraction of college still remained the female crowd. I was proud that my college was at the centre of the Mumbai University and students from all directions—north, south, east, and west—flocked in there. My college was like a dream come true for me. Then suddenly when I saw Paramjeet ... it was like somebody who had slapped me hard to wake me up!

'Fuck, you asshole', I thought. But wait a minute ... from where did Paramjeet land in my dream college. Is he too here or was I still dreaming? I prayed to God for the later one being true but luck was not with me and I was not heard! Paramjeet was standing right in front of me with a huge grin on his face.

'Hello,' he greeted and I returned him a forced smile indicating my displeasure but he was too dumb to understand that. Why did God have to do this to me, I cried. But I guess it was not God's fault, it was the reservation quota. The damn quota system!

'Are you commuting from home daily?' I asked to continue the conversation.

'No ways, we have shifted nearer. What about you?'

'I am staying with my friends in Sector 17, Sai Prasad.'

'Really, that's where my seniors Pondy and Cherry stay. Do you know them?'

'Yeah, actually ... I stay with them.' Can't believe it, now he might visit my place. too, I need a new room, I thought.

'Beware of them; there are so many stories about them floating all around. Though they are very intelligent, they're real-time maniacs!' his advice scared me a bit.

Paramjeet's words were haunting my mind, as I sat to analyse the events that had occurred in the last couple of days. I missed Amar so much. I peeped inside their room through the key hole and to my surprise I realised that the door wasn't locked. Both were not at home either ... it was my golden chance to investigate the whole matter. I decided to sneak in.

I was shocked to see what I found. There were strange instruments scattered all over besides, there was a small gas stove, few other types of burners, and fishy looking chemicals stored in different jars. A foul smell emanated from the room which gave me a headache. The chemicals and the smell suggested that these guys were preparing liquid bomb. I hurried out to call the police ... but ...

'What happened, why you're so restless? Is everything okay?' Pondy started in his usual diplomatic style.

'Actually, your door was not locked and I thought you were in.'

'So, what did you see?' he asked, lighting a cigarette.

'Nothing.'

'Really, then you must see. Please, come in,' he pushed me in. Though he was short and stout he was really very strong. My heart was beating fast, as the thought of my doom hit my head. On the other hand, he was rather calm. He picked some long thing, lying on the floor and hid it behind his shelf.

'What are you thinking?' he said.

'Nothing, sorry, please let me go. I promise I won't tell anybody,' I pleaded with him.

'Hey man, what's wrong with you? Why are you so scared?' he comforted me.

'See, it was a mistake, I didn't mean to ... I wouldn't utter anything about this to anyone, trust me.'

'Like what? What are you saying?

'About the liquid bomb,' I blurted.

'What? Liquid bomb?' he demanded. I pointed towards the rod, he dumped behind. He sat silent for a moment and burst out laughing.

'Fuck ... you bastard! Do I look like a terrorist to you?' he exclaimed, still laughing while I was gazing at him apprehensively. 'That's a pressure gauge.'

'Really?' I still had a doubt. 'What do you do with that?'

'Well my friend, that's another story, he excused himself saying it. However, I still insisted on knowing.

'These things are all used to make bio-diesel, fuel from wastes and are eco-friendly. We stole everything from the college labs and then did some research and even carried out a few experiments. And finally, we succeeded in making it!'

'Wow! That's great! You're genius. I guess this may create a revolution around. Does anybody know about this wonder?'

'Not really bro, we use it to cook food. You see, it's so difficult for students to get kerosene and gas,' he looked at my face which had a dirty expression on. 'We're plastic and polymer engineers, we don't believe in wonders. We create beyond it,' he justified.

My first affair

'Oh! when I look back now
That summer seemed to last forever
and if I had the choice
ya—I'd always wanna be there
Those were the best days of my life.'

The only thing that comes first to my mind whenever I think of my first year in college are the parties we had every night with friends and when life meant just fun and enjoyment. Amey and Amar were always there with me though we were in separate colleges. I even made some new friends here. I avoided going back home even on weekends. Vivek (Pondy) made sure I didn't miss my Mom's cuisines, thanks to his bio-diesel, of course. Trust me, he had some amazing recipes to serve and even more interesting tales to narrate. I loved interacting with him.

'Don't tell me, you're not from Pondicherry?' I grumbled.

'Yeah, I am from Chindwara, Madhya Pradesh. My name is Vivek Pandey.'

'Really? But then why do you have this accent?'

'Well bro, that's another story,' Vivek always began his tales with that line. 'I met with Cherry; his real name is Chiranjeevi when I was in the first year. Like others from his place, he was dumb, arrogant and alien to Hindi, so was always alone. But he had something which attracted me.'

'What?' I cried.

'You dirty mind! Not that way, he had all notes from his seniors, so I made a deal with him—I would be helping him with his Hindi and in return he should share the notes with me. We became friends and stayed together. Now, see what happened after that, courtesy him, I forgot my own Hindi. We are now Pondi + Cherry.

'Cherry is so nasty these days. I gave everything to our friendship, and in the process I think I even lost my identity, friends and career but he doesn't seem to care at all, in turn he has become dumber and even more arrogant. You know how? (I nodded). Because that's again another story ...' he waited for his memory to retrieve the files of flashback. 'He took micro-xerox copy of every beat, yet sometimes didn't even know which answers were for which questions. So, he always asked me, though I hated that since he stocked the chits in his underwear I used to oblige for our friendship. I was caught once for helping him find the right one. I was suspended for a year while he was spared because our HOD was from Pondicherry too. I flunked and he passed and got that bloody teacher job and now wants me to call him Sir, can you believe that?'

'That's really mean of him,' I said.

'Now the latest buzz is that Cherry and our HOD are a couple!' he whispered.

'Really?' I was shocked to hear this.

'Yeah! She has been alone since a long time, ever since her husband committed suicide. Some even say that she was responsible for her husband's death. All these lone years have made her a despo ... I guess and Cherry is just taking all the advantage ... he gets increments and promotions every month, for what ... it's obvious. He must be giving her his*** ... I don't want to say. You know what I mean,' Pondy continued ... and all this made me hate Cherry all the more from the bottom of my heart. There were obvious reasons for that, he used my heater without my permission, never returned a smile and caught my chits twice. A car's noise attracted my attention and I peeped outside the window. It was Amey with a large carton. I wondered what it might be. Two minutes later, the door bell rang and I got my answer.

'From where and why ... a L.C.D. projector?' I asked.

'It's a *sarkari* property *yaar*, my Dad got it from his office and I stole from him. So, don't worry at all,' he said and moved around to arrange the whole stuff. With our little help, it was finally fixed.

'Hurray! Our personal theatre was all set for its first show. Let's celebrate, dude,' Amey cheered and took out the beer bottles from his bag. He had arrived fully prepared for a party. We pulled down all the curtains, laid out our mattress and comforted ourselves among the cushions. Instead of a *mujra*, a porn was entertaining the *babus* of the *mehfil!*

'Does it really pain that much or is she over-reacting?' I said, seeing the blonde damsel in distress.

'C'mon, don't ask me that. You must know it, forgot about that night,' Amey replied.

'Please, buddy, don't remind me about that night. She was a bitch howling all night. It was a nightmare, not again. But tell me, I am a bit confused from the girl's side, what's so fun for them, I mean ... it must be very painful,' I said.

'Who told you that? They enjoy it even more than us or at least as much as us. See, when your ear itches and you put your finger in to scratch, it's a relief and satisfaction for the ear or for the finger?' Amey questioned.

'Obviously, for the ear', I answered as a matter of fact.

'There you are my friend ... so you see the relief and satisfaction is both theirs ... now you understand?' Amey asked.

'Oh!' What a way to explain, I thought! Nobody could beat Amey in that!

'Anyway, how is your college going on?'

'It is fun, I'm enjoying it.'

'Enjoying? Wow! In what sense, *Beta billi mar li kya?*'

'What do you mean?'

'I mean ... a girlfriend, what else, you stupid?'

'No *yaar*, hard luck!'

'Really?'

'Yeah, it's true *yaar*. Nobody seems to be interested in me any more!

'Do you know something, Sam; you're the biggest loser in life if you don't have girlfriend in college. It's something more embarrassing than being caught by your sister!'

'Well, I think there is one girl,' I replied with a ray of hope appearing in my mind.

'C'mon, that would be the *behenji* of your college, the topper of class, she never bunks classes and is the teacher's pet, right?' he was as quick as a lightening.

I was flabbergasted. 'How do you know that? But ... she is pretty, sweet and smart too.'

'Oye, we want her to be hot and not pretty, we want her to be sexy and not sweet. Believe me, girls are better as stupid only and not smart. And anyway, do you want to be called as the *Bhaiyaji?*

(I shook my head.) Don't worry, I'll take your case but on one condition, you have to take her to bed, Amey said rather rhetoric. Yet, don't know why ... I gave my nod.

'What's her name?'

'Shruti.'

'Welcome Shruti to Amey's world,' Amey declared.

In the bed, I was thinking obviously about my soon-to-be girlfriend, I never doubt Amey's instincts. I rewinded to the day when I first met her, the first day of the college, of course. Soon after the first lecture, she stood up and what followed was a long session of queries. She didn't stop nagging the class teacher until she got all answers. Her query sessions continued after every lecture and no doubt, she was soon noticed and was declared the C.R. of the class for scoring 90% in HSC; she seemed visibly happy and more worried for taking up the big post. The very next day she got involved in an argument with the whole class, actually she took this whole C.R. thing quite seriously and was very strict on common-offs. No doubt, the whole class revolted against her and she had to quit. I was one of the pioneers in the movement, so I was pretty sure for the plan not materialising, from my side though; yet I had full faith on Amey.

'Hi!' I greeted. 'I guess the test was fine.' Though I knew it wasn't from her face. She didn't answer me; I thought of trying some of Amey's tips but relented.

'Hello, Samarth' (Wow! She knew my name, I was overjoyed within.) 'The paper was not good at all. I couldn't attempt question no. 10', she replied sadly.

'You might have tried no. 8, that was a bit lengthier but much easier,' I advised casually.

'Yeah, I know that. I had solved that too and it really ate up much of the time and I missed the other one,' she said and punched her fist on the wall in frustration. Where we never bothered for the compulsory questions, there was a girl who was crying in despair for leaving an extra question; too boring.

I was given a small script which I enacted after that. The conversation was something like a disguised survey of her life but she didn't understand at all. Perhaps, she seemed quite frank and tried peeping into my life too. I though, avoided them smartly and bid her bye soon, she acknowledged with a big grin.

Amey had become a regular visitor after we transformed our hall into a mini Porn Theatre, that day Amar too came along. We sat together analysing my chances with Shruti from the observations drawn for the first experiment.

'I told you to say "hello" and not "hi".'

'Well … what's the difference,' I defended.

'No, you idiot!' Amey screamed at me. 'You see, "hello" is something gentlemen type and your "hi" is a straight loser.' However, I still thought, there was no difference in both words. I listened to his nonsense patiently, anyway.

'I am helping him to buy a date and he is not at all serious. I cannot work like this. You have to strictly follow all my instructions or else I am out of it, understood?' he thumped his authority. I nodded.

'She is from Kerala. She stays with her Auntie's family. She had always studied in all-Girls institutes, co-education was something new for her and she was finding it difficult to adjust. She was feeling lonely here and was happy that I talked to her,' I gave away all the details; I collected from my morning survey.

'Wow! You're really lucky,' Amey screamed in joy. 'Trust me; this is going to be the easiest chick ever. Just fuck and forget, dude. And this time Sam, you're going to buy your own condom.'

My next aim was to get her phone number, but not directly. Amey insisted that she should give it to me on her own and that I should not ask for it. So, my job was to create a situation which I did quite easily. I related my enmity with M-series in Maths and she was happy to help, and in the process gave me her number. She also advised me not to hesitate calling her up and that I could call her anytime.

In a couple of days next, I came too close to her, thanks to Amey's tips. I soon introduced her to Amey and she too, like every other girl, was smitten by his persona. In our company, she gradually renovated her black and white life, thanks again to Amey, yet he always gave the credits to me. She finally learned to bunk classes, lied for movies, made friends and stopped bothering the extra questions in papers. In her new *avtar,* she carried all the glory for which our female crowd was famous for, yet nothing between us changed that much and we were still *"just friends".*

'Red rose?' she asked out of surprise. I knew that wouldn't work. But Amey was adamant on it.

'Actually, yellow roses are given for friendship on this day but I consider you are more than that and above yellow it's red,' I elucidated her doubt, the dialogues by Amey of course.

'I guess even I feel the same for you,' she said with a cute smile and gave me one red rose too. Mission accomplished, I cried to myself.

ॐ

It was my turn to call her that day but I completely forgot. Amar had brought a college scandal clip and we were all glued to see the consequence of having a boyfriend with a handycam. I found twenty missed calls on my cell, when I checked after the show. I immediately called Shruti back.

'Sorry, actually we were just moving a watchi ... oops ... I mean watching a movie,' I fumbled; the clip had addled my senses. She wholeheartedly laughed; she even enjoyed some of Amar's worst PJs, quite incredible.

'I was getting bored at home actually. Can I join too?' she asked reluctantly. I don't know what was in my mind but I nodded instantly. Though I realised my mistake after I hung up but it was too late.

'Fuck off Sam, have you gone crazy?' Amar shouted when he learnt of our conversation. But we were good family guys and believed in *Atithi Devo Bhava*.

It was not the first time Shruti was visiting us; we had most of our maths studies at my place only. I even showed her a couple of movies, she had developed a liking for the Bollywood movies, especially the SRK ones and fully enjoyed them. But it was a different situation that day, our heads had gone erotic and we had to host a lady who was undauntingly looking quite sensual in a light blue outfit.

I had promised the classic *Devdas* long time. Two and half hour later, she was spell-bounded by the magical performance of SRK while I was mesmerised by the dusky beauty sitting beside me. I looked at Amey and Amar, they had all slid under the quilts, I knew they were going tizzy too, yet they pretended well. The movie was long and ended late; her aunty had already called twice. She requested me to drop her home and I didn't think twice. Amey whispered to me my next move as I left.

It was just ten and the streets were not empty at all. I didn't know what was going in her mind but all I was searching was for a chance to go ahead with the plan and finally I got it. We stopped at the parking of her building to say good night and then I was to leave. But we stayed mum waiting for the other to initiate, exactly the same what Amey advised. That was the time, I knew it and she knew it too. But then why couldn't I kiss her? What was stopping me? It was weird hanging like that out there and ... and hand and ... Hang!

'Thanks for the movie, I loved it. SRK is awesome,' she said. I knew it was too soon, but I didn't want to miss the chance and pecked my lips over hers. She stayed still though; I couldn't guess what that meant. Did I do it right? I didn't know, I had nothing to compare with or might be I had one, remember the pub night.

'I must go now, Good Night,' she said looking down shyly and left.

Back at my place, Amey and Amar were waiting for me patiently.

'How was it, Romeo?' Amey asked.

'It was good ... it was great, fine, I think,' I replied coldly and went to bed.

Next day, I was wrecked up all over again. I was playing the moment again and again over my head. Was it really too fast, too hard? Did she want me to kiss her? I didn't have an idea. She didn't come to college also. I called her many times to apologise but she didn't pick. I was restless, I couldn't wait anymore and I visited her.

'Hello!' I greeted as she opened the door. She was not expecting me at all, I reckoned from her expression. But I wanted to talk.

'What happened to your phone? Why didn't you come to college today? Are you okay?' I shot all my questions at her while she waited for me to finish.

'Actually, my aunty and uncle are out to some friend's place. So, I stayed home to look after my cousin, he is just seven. And sorry, actually I didn't check my phone at all.'

'Okay, but at least you should have called me. I was so worried.'

'Why?' she grumbled. And yes, why was I worried actually? I didn't have an answer. I looked at her eyes which still demanded explanation, I hung my head down.

'I love you, Sam.'

I couldn't believe my ears, I looked up to check. It was just me and Shruti around. Before I could react, she pulled my head to hers and surprised me with a smooch. It was something different from my previous experience, I was enjoying it and didn't want it to end but she pushed me back.

'Sorry tiger, my cousin is in the bathroom.'

It's all over

'C'mon Amey, can't we go to some other place. See, it's so near to my college. And I am telling you, she is not of that type, she is a good girl,' I requested but as usual it was turned down.

'Have some guts, damn! And don't tell me that she is good or whatever, I know better than you. You'll need it soon; she is a *despo kinda* girl. Just see her past, she has never been so close to a guy and now she is dying for it, you just fuck and forget. In that case, I want you to be prepared, that's it, I am your friend, *na*?' He said as if I don't know how much he cares for me. Fuck you, Amey.

I went up to the shop; the owner was busy far inside reaching for the products the customers demanded. There were five of them excluding me; I thought to wait till all leave but in another five minutes two more arrived. It was the only medical shop around, so there was no way that I could be alone there, I had to dare. And finally our eyes met.

'Condom, please,' I said in a very low tone.

'What, kid? Speak louder,' the owner shouted. Fuck you, asshole. I am capable enough of producing a kid now, how can he call me a kid. I waited for my turn again and this time I made it.

'I want a condom,' I said boldly while others around looked at me in astonishment as if I had asked for AK-47. The owner smiled. He came up to me with a box.

'Vanilla, strawberry ...' now what's that, I wondered as he continued with more flavours, am I in the wrong shop? Actually, I was completely oblivious of the fact that the stuff came in flavours too and hence was jumbled for what to choose and what to say, both. The owner understood.

'First time, dude?' he patted my shoulder with a naughty smile.

'Try strawberry. (Wow! What flavours, I thought!) It's very popular these days,' he suggested, my face still perplexed while others giggled lowly. 'Use condom' is what government promotes, something expected from responsible citizens and that was what I was doing. What was so funny then?? I don't understand. Now, that's actually people's narrow-mindedness and small thinking, the exact reason why we are lagging behind the Western world, I mean both the poor thinking and the non-use of condoms.

It had been six months since Shruti said those three magical words to me. Amey's predictions went all wrong, I was still waiting for the big bonanza and was fed up of carrying condoms in my pockets, though we kissed each other, moved around hand-in-hand and watched flop movies together in corner seats of empty theatre but sex was yet only in my fantasies. However, in this brief period we had come really close to each other that we could not stay separated; we spend most our time at college together, yet our call rates both in terms of frequency and money had increased. I realised that she was a good girl and loved me very much yet I was to spoil her, I was feeling a bit guilty, after all I am a good boy. But then, Amar came up with a fantastic quote on his T-shirt yet again.

Intelligent Man + Intelligent Woman = Romance
Stupid Man + Intelligent Woman = Affair
Intelligent Man + Stupid Woman = Pregnancy
Stupid Man + Stupid Woman = Marriage

The strange calculations kept buzzing in my mind and I thought to explore my romance for a few more days considering that both of us were intelligent.

∾

The result of the first semester was out, mine was an average effort but I had no ATKTs, quite shockingly I had scored well in M-I and electrical. Why will it not be? Shruti had topped in the class, the combined studies, the library sessions, the discussions and her notes proved to be a jackpot. There are real good advantages of having a smart and intelligent girlfriend. Sorry Amey, I think this time you're wrong, I was happy that she was not stupid like Amey's girls are always.

The college ended early that day, a few wanted to celebrate and most were to regret. I offered Shruti to come to my place to celebrate, of course, with another romantic movie and she agreed happily. Shruti's Aunty had a doubt regarding us and the exams made our *after college romance* take a backseat for some time. In the vacations she went to Kerala so it was after a long time that we were together. Whether for the result or the long separation, I don't know but she was undoubtedly looking charming and equally lovable. I kissed her straightaway knowing that others were not at home and she kissed back too. Those happy moments inspired me to sing and make it even more special. I took out my guitar and music diary after a long time. I had never told her about my passion for music and as expected she couldn't believe it.

'Sam, what are you doing?' she grumbled as I tried on a few chords to get my touch back.

'Now, shut up please and listen to this,' I bawled. I took my music diary and:

Sometimes at night,
When I lay down to sleep,
I embrace myself,
I start to think ...
Then I imagine
That you lie beside me ...
Hugs and kisses
All over my body.
I wish you
Could really be here,
Just to whisper,
'I love you,' in my ear.
I would turn around and say,
'I love you, too.'
But will it ever be true?
So, I turn around
And I wonder some more,
Still wanting your embrace,
So, I close my eyes and picture your face ...
I fall asleep dreaming of you.
In my dream it seems so true.
It's as if I can really feel
Your kisses against my lips ...
Then my eyes pop open

And you're nowhere to be seen,
And I feel so lonely
Once AGAIN!

I finished my song and looked at her, expecting a round of applause but she was all dumbfounded with the same expression which I had when I had watched a porn film for the first time. I shook her.

'Everything okay?' I asked and she nodded.

'Wow! I never knew, my boyfriend was so talented. You must try for 'Indian Idol' this year. Tell me one thing frankly, did you write the song, too?,' she asked me excitedly.

'Yeah, of course.' I lied. 'I wrote it for you. It's all because of our love dear, that a dork like me has turned a poet. I love you.' Actually I had found that song once on a piece of paper in a book at the library. I give the person special thanks for it, straight from my heart. At least, somehow and somewhere it worked and created wonders, and I could see that in Shruti's sparkling eyes.

'I love you too,' she giggled and came closer to me. Our lips were just a couple of centimetres apart when her phone howled from the table, a very weird ring for a girl. She rose to answer it.

'Maybe, today I would be lucky.' I thought as I checked my pockets for the condoms, still a week before it expires, I calculated.

'What is that?' she grunted and I fumbled to hide the packet.

'Everything okay?' she asked in doubt and I sheepishly nodded, putting it under the pillow. 'Sam, I can't believe it, I'm in love. I never planned nor do I know how it happened. But now, our love has become my plan for life and my reason for living,' she was really going filmy, I thought but who cares for that. I continued our love from where she left, kissing, hugging and *bubbling* but she had to interrupt again for a dialogue.

'Sam, do you know love is one of the hardest things because you have many thoughts that can't be expressed.'

'And do you know exams are still harder because you don't have any thoughts, still you have to express and I have succeeded in doing so. It took more than thirty sleepless nights, no fun, no love, tonnes of labour to mug up useless derivation and theories, even more efforts to vomit it on paper to clear it. And all I want now is love from you, honey,' I yelled out of disgust. I think that was really something mean to say, but she was still ...

'Sorry,' she was shocked though. 'I know Sam, how much you love me. I am all yours,' she said with a *take me in your arm look*, that was what I was waiting for desperately but the way she said that, something pricked my mind. I couldn't go ahead, I gazed at her innocent face thinking how to get out of it and this time, I was heard. The door bell rang, somebody was outside. I ran to open the door, happily.

'Hi' it was Pondy, I had never felt so happy seeing him ever. He looked at me suspiciously. What a great timing, Pondy!

ϖ

I threw the condom packet in the dustbin and went to bed but couldn't sleep at all. I tried even harder, yet couldn't rest my mind. The thoughts of Shruti were haunting my mind; I was feeling a strong guilt inside my mind. I was doing all wrong to her, I realised. It was all love from her side and all I was thinking of was just sex. Why Shruti, being so intelligent you had to be so dumb not to understand the evil in me, I thought. To hell with Amey's *Fuck n Forget* policy, I couldn't do it to her; I would tell everything to her the next morning, I decided.

'Hey! Sam,' it was Pondy. I hate people calling me at my back. I returned him a furious look.

'How was she, anyway? You know ... what I mean. She's hot and sexy, you're lucky, dude,' he said toasting the condom packet which I had thrown other night. My fury grew into rage over his lines and I hurled him to the wall ferociously.

'Mind your own business, asshole,' I warned him and left.

I sat at the canteen waiting for Shruti to come, but she didn't come, instead her SMS struck my phone.

'Come to my home right now. I have a surprise for you.'

I thought for a second, what the surprise might be. Had her aunty come to know about me or she is ... no way, we had just kissed. I couldn't think of any more possibilities, my brain was already messed up and I rushed to her place.

'Hi' I said as she opened the door with an enchanting smile.

'What happened?' I shouted.

'Calm down, tiger, what's wrong with you?'

'No, what's wrong with you, tell me. Why did you call me here?' I was still restless.

'Everything okay sweetie, nothing is wrong. My whole family is out for the whole day and I thought why not use the day for some real fun,' she said with a sedative effect and cuddled around my arm. I knew about her intention and drew her aside immediately.

'What?' she grunted.

'No, Shruti, I cannot do this,' I paused for a moment and looked at her face; she seemed totally baffled over my behaviour. I took a long breath and spat the truth.

'I lied to you all these days. I don't love you Shruti. Amey had all planned our love story, I just followed his instructions. We had already made detailed notes about you and I behaved accordingly. I just wanted to have some fun with you. So I did all these things. I am sorry but that's the truth.'

Silence had crept through the room after my confession. I couldn't dare to look at her face, I hung my face down. I knew she was hurt.

'So, why are you telling me all this now?' she said with a broken voice.

'Because I care for you ...'

'Don't you dare say that,' she interrupted.

'Now, get out from here,' she shouted, her eyes filled with tears.

'See Shruti, I know I did wrong but can't we forget everything and start our life in a different and better way. We can be close friends forever,' I tried to console.

'Fuck off, Sam. Hell with you and your friendship. You all men are bastards. Now please, leave me alone,' she sobbed.

I understood it was over now, I broke her heart and she wouldn't forgive. It would be better for both of us, if we stayed away from each other.

'Sam', she screamed my name. I turned, she ran at me. A tight slap was what I was expecting and I closed my eyes. But it was just a soft peck from her lips. I looked at her surprisingly.

'I need to thank you for giving me, my best days. Thank you,' she said and trembled in tears.

Now I had some relief and was content that we called it off at the right time. I didn't deserve her love, I implied to myself.

'I am not ready for any commitment right now,' I excused.

'Cool! I like that, Sam,' Amey grunted. 'So, need a drink to flush it off your mind completely?'

'No thanks, its okay,' I searched for Pondy, I needed to apologise. He was in his room, mixing chemicals to create fuel for his stove. Morning assault was still in his mind, he completely ignored me. I advanced towards him.

'I am sorry,' I said but he didn't acknowledge my presence. 'I am sorry,' I reiterated. He looked at me for a moment and then continued again with his experiments. I drew back to the hall.

'I'm making *Paneer Tikka* tonight, anybody interested?' he yelled at my back. I turned back to give him a tight hug.

The Failure

Sometimes, I really missed Shruti a lot, especially while solving M-II and searching for missing views and hidden curves in ED. On the other hand, I knew Shruti felt the same. I can say that to fill the emptiness in our lives we both reverted to our first love again, she books and me guitar. She got back to her shell again, away from this cruel and selfish world, studying and studying even more. I also spent most of my time playing with my old six-string, and visited Rasayani frequently.

'It's easy to turn friendship into love and impossible to turn love into friendship. If two past lovers remain friends, they are either still in love or were never in love,' Shalini asserted, though there was no doubt in my mind the dialogue came through a forwarded SMS. Perhaps, I hate myself for the fact that why the hell did I ever tell my story to everybody. I mean, it gives my mind a sting all over again, I am really a fool.

'What about you Shalini? Still single?' I changed the topic.

'Why man? Don't you think I am beautiful too?' she said giving a girlie pose and I returned her a dirty look.

'You're mean. Anyway his name is Prashant, senior to me.'

'Wow! But I guess he matches your height.'

'Of course, you idiot! Perhaps he is taller even, the most handsome guy of our college and very sweet too. Sometimes, I feel that perfect men do exist. I am in love. I don't believe on this boyfriend concept and all, he is my true love and not my friend or something. And, he really appreciates my thoughts,' she said showing off her sparkling earrings at me, gift from her new boyfriend, oh! sorry, true love. I regretted, asking her about that, as she went on and on with her romance tale and I needed a change of topic again.

'Hey! 'Indian Idol' is back,' I exclaimed seeing the ad on TV. 'It went rocking last season. Abhijeet Sawant is a star now. I was waiting for it to return, long time.'

'Why don't you try this year, you will do well. I will vote for you.'

'C'mon, if you vote I will lose definitely. Remember, last time you voted for Amit Sana and he lost,' I joked.

'Sam, jokes apart, I am serious. You've been learning music since a long time, I am sure you can make it big. Even Abhijeet was an underdog in life before this and look at him now.'

'What underdog? I am not the one, understand.'

'C'mon Sam, nobody knows you better than me. You don't know how talented you are. You are a bloody jerk ...' Shalini had started again. I knew there was no point in arguing, I can never win against her.

The 'Indian Idol' topic never got off my mind after that. I had always dreamt of becoming a rock star and 'Indian Idol' was just the perfect platform for me. I decided to at least give it a try and checked on all the updates about it regularly. I practised daily on the guitar to get my lost touch back. I didn't want anyone to mock at me, so I kept it a secret. But as per my nature, I was always double minded while taking big decisions and I couldn't select a final song for the audition, I needed my friends.

'Try Breathless,' Amey prompted. 'It's a wonderful song; the judges would be surely impressed by it.'

'Man! How can I sing that? Perhaps, nobody can actually, even the original singer didn't. It was same as cut and take shot like thing.'

'Chaiya, Chaiya, try that. It's funky and cool,' Amar's choices were always cheap as him.

'Fuck! You bastards! I did a mistake by asking you about it, I shouted in disgust.

My friends know about music as much as Zyed Khan knows about acting. I had to do it all alone, it would be rather better, I thought. I decided on the genre first, I should go with something that suits my style, I implied. I preferred going for a slow rock song, after a couple of hours of immense searching, I finalised Bhulado Acoustic.

And finally came the dates of the both auditions and my exams too. The Mumbai audition clashed with my M-II paper, my Mom would kill me if I skipped my paper, so there was no way that I was going there. But then, I couldn't let off my dreams that easily and this time Amey came with yet another bold and dodgy idea.

'But I don't know anybody there. Moreover, I've never been there too,' I protested immediately.

'Abe, ladki dekne jaa raha hai kya?' Amey scolded. 'You will just give audition and come back after that. See, after the Maths paper there is a five-day gap before the next one. The Ahmedabad audition is two days later, so no doubt, you can return from the audition and still would have enough time to study. Most importantly, nobody would come to know about it also. It's just perfect.'

His plans always looked simple on paper but were far risky in reality. But I didn't have any other alternative too. I had to go for it.

ɷ

I had solved integrals and traced trajectory all night, yet I couldn't squeeze those steps from my mind. The musical symbols were all going over my head. I tried my best to overcome, yet I could just recollect the lyrics of my audition song ... *Bhulado bhulado yeh baatein purani.* My brain was completely screwed up and I was scotched. I submitted the paper and came outside. However, I was not bothered much about it. I maintained a fake smile to avoid my friends knowing about the paper. I was just concerned about the audition.

I reached Ahmedabad at 9.00 a.m. It was a long and tiring twelve-hour journey. I had not slept in the bus, maybe because of the excitement or because of the Indian roads. I checked my cell, a couple of messages from friends wishing me luck. I was lucky enough to have such good friends, I smiled at the thought. I knew what really my success meant to them. I took a rickshaw and left for the audition venue. After reaching there, I realised it was just not me who wanted to be the next Abhijeet by seeing the one kilometre long line. I too joined the line all the same.

'So, you want to participate in *Indian Idol?*' I thought of starting a conversation with the guy standing ahead of me.

'No, I am standing for ration,' he replied, while others mocked at me. Bloody asshole!

The line was moving at a snail's pace. Our patience was tested at its best. I was feeling hungry, weary and sleepy, standing for hours. My face had turned pale, head was blasting and eyes were burning red. I looked around; everyone's condition almost was similar to mine. The excitement and the passion to be the next heartthrob of India had all gone down, yet nobody was ready to walk out.

'Excuse me, I think I need to go the toilet. Will you please see my line till I come back?' it was the same guy standing in front. 'I think I need to ...' he just ran saying this!

'Hey! Thanks!' he said after returning, I nodded reluctantly. 'Are you still thinking about that? See, I was kidding *yaar*. Chill *yaar*. What's your name?'

'Sam.'

'My name is Sandy, friends?' he said and brought his hands forward. It reminded of someone whom I adore so much. I smiled back and we shook hands.

'So, Sam. You want to be the next 'Indian Idol', right?'

'No, standing for ration,' I smiled and he grimaced.

'Jokes apart, I'm serious.'

'Of course ... damn! That's why everyone is here,' I said point-blankly.

'Not me. Actually, I am interested in politics. Look, these days popularity is what matters there and I think 'Indian Idol' is just one of the best ways to gain it. Once I get popular through the show, I will jump into politics. You see, it gonna help me a lot. Moreover, the voting system will prepare me for the big time ... He continued with his big plans while I just closed my ears to whatever he said. I wanted to laugh but that would have hurt his sentiments, I controlled with a lot of difficulty of course.

Finally, my chance came as Sandy returned jumping outside the green room. He was selected, I congratulated him and he wished me luck before he left. I had not eaten anything and was feeling very weak and dizzy, but I kept telling myself that I am gonna be popular and boosted my confidence. It was imminent that I would be selected for sure. I entered the room in style.

'Good afternoon,' I greeted the judges.

'It's evening, my friend,' one of them said, checking his watch.

'Sorry,' I said while the judge gestured me to continue. I took out my bag for my guitar.

'Excuse me, guitar is not allowed. Don't you know the rules?'

'But!'

'Don't argue. Please!' they ordered.

My guitar had always been my companion while I sang. Leaving it aside was like a setback, the pain which had vanished, got over me again. I started my song but was all faulty. My mind fumbled and I missed notes, words, I was completely out of scale and committed many other fatal mistakes, too.

'This is 'Indian Idol' and not a society gathering, what are you doing here, boy?' The judges gave their opinion.

'Sir, I beg of you to give me another chance,' I pleaded.

'What? There are still hundreds of people waiting and you want a second chance?'

I started singing again from the beginning, I made a good start but could not hold on to the notes, I was used to my guitar support for the flow and again in the middle I forgot the lyrics. I tried again but knew it won't, so I stood mum in the middle while judges were constantly gaping at me. I was out, I knew.

'See, I understand what you're feeling? But tell me what you would have done if you were in our place?' the lady judge said with a disappointed note. I didn't answer her; all of a sudden tears came running down my eyes. It was the worst moment of my life and I truly didn't deserve.

ॐ

My practice and hard work had gone in vain, my hopes drowned and my dreams were all shattered in just a moment. The world had come to an end for me. I had lost everything there; I could not hold back my tears. I was in the bus. The beautiful sight across the window, unlike other times didn't attract me in the least bit instead, I was searching for my own image in the glass and was feeling all lost. I was broken from inside. I tried to sleep but couldn't. It was straight two days, and I had not even slept one wink.

'Hey! Sam, what happened?' Pondy opened the door. I avoided him and went straight to my room. Pondy sensed something was wrong and called for others.

Within half an hour, Amey and Amar arrived. My door was locked from inside and they were howling and knocking hard. I wanted to stay alone and ignored them which only created panic among them. They became more concerned and put in more efforts to get in. I had got an idea what these three idiots might be thinking and didn't want to gather the neighbours. I opened the door and there came all three of them tumbling over each other.

'Fuck, what are you guys up to?' I shouted.

'You're alright, *na*?' Amar checked with me. 'Thank God! We thought ...

'No way Amar, I can't do that. I'm a loser and coward.'

Amey slapped me. 'Asshole, just shut up. It's just a bloody show. Forget it, that's not the end, it means nothing *yaar*. There is always a next time and do you think ending life is the solution. Think about your parents and what about us, damn!'

He gave me a tight hug and Pondy and Amar also ran to hug me. I couldn't control my tears. The competition meant a lot to me and couldn't get out of it completely. The scene of audition kept on haunting my mind over and over. I couldn't concentrate on anything and in the process screwed my rest of the papers too.

I deduced it was all my fault. Mom was right in her own way; I was playing with my career. I shouldn't have given priority to the competition at all. But then, the mistake was already committed and I knew how grave the consequences would be. I planned my cover. In the next few days of my vacation, I tried my level best to cajole my parents before the results were out. I obeyed everything they said, never argued on TV programmes, cleaned my room daily and always kept the glass in the basin after finishing my milk. My Mom did raise her eyebrows seeing the change but was happy.

The results were out and I realised I had committed a sin and not a mistake. I failed that year with four ATKTs. As expected it was boom-boom from Mom, Dad was quiet but his silence conveyed many things. I accepted my fault and was ready to improve. But everything had changed; I could not retrieve the time and the faith which I had lost. The failure tag was imposed on me forever.

I got into depression for some time. Rarely, I talked to someone. I had isolated myself from all my friends, no calls, no outings, nothing. I spent most of my time in my room just browsing through my past and repenting on my foolishness. I cried and cried even more. I was fed up of life. Many times, I got this strong urge to end my life but I didn't have that courage to slit my veins. But then, would it really end all my pain, I thought. I didn't know, what about my parents? Why should they suffer for my deed? I had to live for them but I need to prove myself first. I'll try and give my best, I promised myself.

I smashed my Guitar first on the wall; no more music in my life. I wouldn't go aimless and wayward any more, only meaningful things would happen around, I got a lot of time with me and would utilise it to the fullest, I decided. Next morning, I got up early, got ready and went to the dining room to have a word with Dad.

He got a bit surprised but stayed calm like most of the days, post-results. But Mom's curiosity paid off and she inquired.

'I am going for an interview. I am seeking a job,' I said boldly.

Adding a new chapter

'Wait outside,' she said. I couldn't make out anything from her expression.

I was sweating in an A.C. room, it was going to be my very first interview. Four or five of us were waiting outside peering through the glass wall; the interview was being conducted inside and a lovely lady was taking it. She was greeting everybody with a bright smile which I could see diminishing as the interviews progressed. Most of them came outside in merry; they were to receive a call soon from the company later. I was wondering about my status, I was asked to wait. My interview was average, I was not sure of it. I was getting impatient sitting there for hours; I had completed reading the whole of *The Times of India* including the Speaking Tree, its other supplements such as Ascent, Bollywood Times and Mumbai Mirror. I skipped page 33 (Ask the Sex Expert) though, to avoid glances and naughty giggles from others but over the years I had almost known the answers to the queries mostly asked!

And finally, I was fed up and moved out. The Telnet office was just above the Vashi railway station. So, in another minute I was waiting again, for a train this time. I checked the time, it was 5.30 p.m., and the train exactly came on time. 'Thank God, I came outside.' I said to myself because in another half hour, it would be rush hour and I hated travelling in crowd. The train was empty and I was lucky, I got a window seat, quite rare for me. To Panvel it was half-an-hour journey by train and still there were 15 minutes for the train to depart, I started feeling sleepy at the thought of it only!

Few minutes later I was shaken off by somebody. I opened my eyes, half. An elderly man was standing in front of me and was saying something; I didn't care and closed my eyes again. He shook me hard this time and I was like completely shocked, my eyes were wide open. For a moment I couldn't recollect anything as I looked around with a jumbled expression. The elderly man waited till I came to senses.

'The young people today have all become lazy and careless,' he cursed. I always wondered why the old generation always had a problem with us, why couldn't they just leave us alone. I ignored his words completely and looked outside the window but he was adamant on speaking to me.

'Hey you! I am talking to you,' he shouted and I returned him a furious look.

'Pick up your phone, you idiot! It's been ringing since long.'

I checked and he was right, yet I felt that there was no reason for him to be so angry and he could have as well minded his own business. I picked up the call and a sweet voice greeted 'hello' followed by my name with an added *'Mr* tag'. Another sales call, no not again, I thought.

'Sorry, I am a student; not earning. Can't help you really,' I said.

'Excuse me, this is Reena from Telnet,' the lady reverted aggressively.

'Sorry again, I made a mistake. Sorry, sorry,' I reiterated desperately.

'It's okay. Where are you? You were here for an interview, right?'

'Yeah, so?'

'Well ... you have been selected and you are supposed to report in another minute or we may consider someone else,' she said and hung up.

My brain cells work slowly in situations like these when one has to decide fast, it took time again for me to get hold of it and I realised I had to rush. The train had already started and the local trains pick up really fast. I didn't wait for my brain to analyse the state of affairs and jumped off it. I had a safe landing, luckily. The other commuters shouted, cursed and lauded at my stunt, I took the compliments wholeheartedly. I always wanted to do something like this and eventually got an opportunity!

∞

'Where were you, Mr Samarth?' Her name was Sandhya Sharma, the HR manager and probably ... the most beautiful boss on earth!

'Actually ma'am, I thought I was not ... my ... my ... interview was not ...' I said sheepishly.

'Well, I understand what you are trying to say, but I want you to work with us. I like you, boy,' she said and napped my hair a bit.

'Here is your offer letter. See you at office from tomorrow then.' She ended with a few more compliments.

I opened the letter in the lift itself. I was to be paid ten thousand bucks per month. I was more shocked than happy, was I worth it, I wondered. At home, I showed the letter to my parents, they were visibly happy for my sake. It didn't hurt me though; I had become a bit sensible to understand their mind, too.

Next morning, I woke up early and got ready silently for my first day at work. I didn't want to disturb anybody and thought of slipping outside quietly. But I couldn't, I realised as I sneaked through my room's door that it wasn't just me who was moving around so early. Mom had already done up with her daily chores and was busy with her regular prayers. Not a big deal though, I ignored and reached for the door but a familiar and sweet aroma held back my steps. I checked on the breakfast table, Mom had really made the day very special for me, it was quite a long time since I relished on *paneer tikka*.

'Thanks, Mom,' I said in bonhomie.

'*Beta,* eat it slowly till I pack your tiffin,' Mom said. What? A tiffin? That also a big one, I mean we always differentiate people in train with this thing. You see, in Mumbai local trains, there are just two kinds of people—working uncles and cool students (but ... no comments about the ladies compartment!). So, carrying the tiffin promoted ... demoted ... to just say put me in the other category.

I boarded the 8.15 a.m. train, slow to C.S.T. that meant a crowded one. Yet, I didn't think of hanging on at the door, like other days. I was like more into my new role and looked in for a seat. No doubt, the friendly commuters adjusted me in a seat which was meant for just three normal butts but was supporting four large ones! I was still holding my bag over my lap which had grown in size too.

'Hey! Why don't you put your bag up? It would be more comfortable,' the elderly man sitting next to me suggested. I smiled at him and he gave me a blank look. But how? The spaces between the seats were also occupied. The person standing in front of me, picked it from my lap and put it up, without even bothering whether I was really willing or not.

Half-an-hour later, I could see the train moving out of Sanpada, my destination was next and I rose to reach at the door. However, I realised my mistake as I looked around. I should have thought about it long time, I regretted. I didn't want to be late on the very first day of my job but did I get a chance to think on it? No. I was pushed in the crowd by my friendly fellow commuters to grab my seat. I was almost to die suffocating and my bones were all getting crushed as I was slipping through that five yards distance to the gate which was no less an experience than fighting with an Anaconda but I eventually managed to escape and survive.

A fifteen-day training was to be attended before we were to hit the main department. I was selected for Secure Life. The security showed me the way to the training hall, quite a cool one, with cubicles made of soft board, swirling and comfortable chairs, and expensive carpet, something much better than what I had expected. There were eight of them, like me, all guys but from different age groups, waiting for our product trainer. I smiled at them and took a seat at the last. In another few minutes our trainer entered, the same beautiful lady who took my interview. She was in her early twenties but married.

'Hey! It's not your college, sit at the front. Trust me, I won't bore you much,' she said with a cute smile. I glanced at her; going by her charismatic appeal, there was no doubt in my mind that she must have been a sex siren in her college days.

'Hello to you all. I am Sandhya Sharma,' she introduced herself. 'I am going to train you before you get into the business.'

Deepak, Masood, Mayur, Pratik, Rakesh, Ravi, Sangam and Swapnil—I got to know the names of my team members, as each one of us gave their brief introduction. After that it was induction which is an introduction about the company like the owners, stocks, shares, product and blah … blah … which never seemed to come to an end as the slides continued to scroll and I was getting damn bored.

'Excuse me, learn to take interest. The company is not paying you to doze,' she shouted, I realised I was caught.

In the break, I splashed water on my face and washed with soap in the wash room. I looked at the mirror, the rest of my team was having a hearty laugh at me. They tried to control as I approached.

'C'mon, it happens. Don't mind it. We're a team, right?' Deepak said. He was the eldest amongst us. He had five years of experience working in call centres and was aware of all terms and laws.

'It seems most of you are freshers,' this time it was Rakesh. 'Let me tell you something. Being in the same team, we need to be together always. It helps a lot in achieving targets.'

We decided to stay always together even in the washroom, no matter how poor, laugh at all jokes of team members, start log in always 10 min late and log out 20 min early, share clients, data and lunch without hesitating and lastly nobody in the team eyes Sandhya since Deepak was clean bowled by the malicious beauty.

'Hey! But she is married,' I protested.

'You kid, know nothing about the BPO culture,' Deepak said.

'BPO, what's that?' I asked.

∽

'Business Process Outsource is the most common term used for call centers,' explained Sandhya … oops … I mean Sandhya Ma'am, sorry Deepak, my tongue slipped.

'There are two types of processes, i.e. Outbound and Inbound … Sandhya Ma'am continued.

'Hey! It's of no use,' Deepak pinned me and said 'Read this,' he gave me his cell to read a Santa–Banta joke. In Amar's company, I had known all of them, yet I produced a fake smile recalling the ultimatum and was caught again.

'It seems you are really going to have a tough time with me,' she warned and I looked down guiltily.

With two more breaks and plenty of blah ... blah ... from Sandhya Ma'am, my first day at job ended. It was not a good one though. I got scolded thrice; I wished my boss didn't believe in the quote that *first impression is the last impression*.

'Mr Samarth, no T-shirts, no jeans, no sandals and no *chappals* allowed.' That was the fourth one, even if she hadn't till then, I was giving her every reason to pull my ears.

But then, that was not the end of my distress. I had missed two trains in a row. Because of the crowd I couldn't board them but was well aware of the fact the rush hours were on till next two hours. So, any how I had to take the risk and reach home clinging to the door. No wonder, why insurance companies pay for useless people like me so much.

He is back

'Mom, are there any wrinkle-free shirts,' I asked and Mom gave me a blank look.

'They're all ironed, *beta*.'

'No, I didn't mean that. Just forget it,' I knew I couldn't explain it. 'I am thinking of staying with my friends again. The journey is too tiring.'

'It's just a single day; you went to the job and you are already complaining,' Mom said.

'It's nothing like that. The job is cool but the travelling sucks,' I bit my tongue. Mom had narrowed her eyes and I returned a sheepish smile.

'Don't know what you people do there. I really won't allow you to go there again.'

'I am not asking you for permission, I am just saying that I'll shift on Sunday. See, I get so tired after the travel that I would hardly be able to study. My friends are there, I will study with them.' I left for my office.

I tried Amey's number a couple of times for the keys but it was not reachable. The flat was empty since Vivek aka Pondy had cleared his exams and Cherry was living in with the HOD. I messaged him about the room and asked him to call back after office. I switched off my cell following the rules and regulations of the company.

I encountered giggles and short laughs all over as I headed for the training room. The giggles and the short laughs turned into big ones as I pushed in the room. I waited for my team to stop but they didn't.

'Hey! What's wrong with you all?'

'What's wrong with us? Haven't you looked at the mirror?'

'Yeah! But why?'

'C'mon, bloody geek; are you wearing your Dad's clothes?'

'No, it's mine and it's a formal type. What's so funny in that? Mom said I look handsome in this.'

They stopped everything instantly hearing this and looked at me in astonishment, before starting it all over again.

'What?'

'You're wearing something of the 70s and asking us, what? It's weird, no it's disgusting. And by the way, look at the colour of your trousers. What colour is it?'

'Maybe, it is greenish grey,' my knowledge about colour is horrible.

'Wow! Thanks, *Mamma's boy.*'

That tag had always irked my mind. I was hurt yet again. But I really couldn't help it, I had grown old hearing it, literally speaking. And off late, had stopped protesting against it as I feel not all people are wrong to say or think of me like that. *I indeed was Mamma's boy!*

'Today, I will show you a short a film. Watch it carefully as I would ask your take on the film individually,' Sandhya Ma'am announced and everyone lauded interestingly. But then, our excitement vanished as the film went on. Actually, it was a documentary on insurance, recalling all difficulties faced by a non-insured family. One hour of complete mental torture.

'So, I will give you five minutes and you guys have to tell me about it in brief, okay!' She said and the rest got busy in drawing notes and conclusion from their observations while I knew doing it first would really give advantage and raised my hand immediately.

'What Mr Samarth? Any doubt?' she asked.

'No. Actually I've finished with it, so can I?'

I rose and went to the front. Everybody was staring at me and the scene reminded me about my Farewell party in school. C'mon, if I could sing in front of hundred odd people, speaking there was not at all a big deal. I cleared my throat and began what Sandhya Ma'am does best—Blah ... blah ... Ten minutes later, they were still looking at me but their mouths were wide open as I completed my explanation.

'Cool! That was just awesome. I am impressed,' she gave me thumbs up and I realised I had hit on the bull's eye straightaway.

'You were very good,' praised Deepak as I returned to my seat.

'C'mon, the *Mamma's boy* is good at something,' I answered in full attitude.

After others finished, Sandhya Ma'am gave us a short break. All of us went to the cafeteria; however, I chose to stay away from the crowd and sat alone, sipping probably the world's worst coffee! The morning training session had tired me completely and I thought it was better to check out some hot chicks than sit and gossip with the rest of the gang. That's when my eyes fell on Jessica; I read the name on her I-card as she passed. I wondered why I hadn't noticed her as yet. But it was really not my fault. She seemed to be pretty shy and talked very less, really? Then what was she doing in a call center. Actually, she was always on call whether officially (clients) or personally (boyfriend). She was very beautiful; no way could she be single. I was disappointed a bit, yet I couldn't stop myself from checking her out! So, for the next couple of days, I followed her everywhere she went, except the washroom of course!

∾

Amey didn't call, so I called him up after office.

'Hello. Where are you? I asked.

'Yeah! I got your message and was going to call you only,' he said. Somebody is already staying there, so I just want to confirm if you are okay with it.'

'Yes, no problem, I will shift on Sunday. Just tell him to stay away from my room.'

'Sam, I insist you come here and meet him once before shifting.'

I had not seen Amey for a long time. Perhaps, I thought watching a movie with him would be better idea than a fight with Mom for the remote. Let her enjoy her *saas-bahu* sagas at home.

'Okay! Let's meet.'

Amey was waiting for me at the society gate, quite a strange thing. Something had to be fishy around, I suspected. Amey tried his best to be normal while I was waiting with baited breath.

'Had a fancy dress competition or what?' he commented looking at my clothes.

'Fuck off,' was my response.

'You can have your room; the other guy will stay in Pondy's room,' his approach was apprehensive.

'So ... you already told me that on phone. I am here to meet him, right?'

'Yeah! But he's out.'

'No problem, dude. I'll wait for him. Let's go in. I don't wish to get home. Today's dinner is on me. But you've to show me a movie then.'

'Sure, I've got Spiderman-3. Anyway, I guess you won't have much problem with your new roommate. He too is from your college, plastic and polymer!'

'Do I know him?' I inquired.

'Yeah! Quite very well,' he said confidently. But something was smothering his mind, I sensed.

'Hey! What's wrong?'

'Sam, you're grown-up now and should learn to forgive. In school, we were all kids and perhaps I think, there is no use in digging up the skeletons of past ...'

'Is all this related to my new roommate?' I interrupted; something flicked my mind as I heard about school and past. I was frantically soothing myself that it could not be true but as my eyes fell on the football, the doubt in me was cleared.

'Paramjeet!' I screamed.

'Cool down, boy.'

'How could you even think that I will stay with him? He's my worst enemy, I hate him.'

'But why? He's really a good guy, trust me. I don't know what really freaks you. He is never cynical about you. You really act so mean.'

'Yeah! I am mean. I won't stay here anymore. I'm leaving.'

'C'mon, don't go. Who's going to pay for my dinner then?'

'It's not funny,' I said in fury.

'Please, let me explain it. Paramjeet is really going through a bad phase in life. He is not staying with his parents anymore. I gave him the room understanding his problem and need. Try or I'll ask him to go.'

'What do you mean by saying *try him?*'

'C'mon, it's not funny either. The flat was empty for a long time and my Dad was pestering me to give it on rent. Anyway, you won't be able to afford the flat alone.'

He was right from his own side. It's really not necessary that we cross our ways; after all, we had separate rooms. I desperately needed a room and it was really difficult to get such a wonderful room at such a rate. So, thinking of all the circumstances, I nodded to take the room ... with the entertainment that Amey provided once in a while, of course!!

'Tell me Amey, this Spiderman-3 CD belongs to Paramjeet, right?'

'Yeah! But how did you know?'

∾

I was still not talking much with my teammates; it was just those formal *Hi's and Hello's* between me and them. Even they had understood that it really hurt me but hadn't apologised yet, so I also didn't make any extra effort from my side either. I tried to concentrate more on Sandhya Ma'am's presentations. I raised doubts, answered questions, prepared presentations, kept updated myself and even demonstrated a few examples with her. My closeness with her did make other people envious but the best trainee award of the month was what I was aiming for, of course, to impress my *Jessi aka Jessica*. I liked to call her that.

'Dude ... you are on the wrong track!' Deepak warned me in the cafeteria.

'Hey! I am not seeing Sandhya, I mean Sandhya Ma'am,' I said.

'I am not talking about her, can you come to the washroom,' he said. But I ignored him because I was smitten by *Jessi* who was as usual, I presumed, talking to her boyfriend on phone.

'I said, come to the washroom,' Deepak shouted from the corner while everybody smirked at me, even Jessi paused from her conversation and looked at me suspiciously. I didn't want Deepak to create a scene, so I quietly got up to go to the washroom.

'What do you think of yourself?' I asked him in anger.

'Chill Samarth, this is not your school,' he said casually leaning at the wall.

'Oh! really, then are you aware of that fact yourself?'

'See, I told you, you're going the wrong way.'

'And I told you already, I'm not seeing Sandhya Ma'am.'

'I am talking about the other girl ... dude.'

'You mean *Jessi*.'

'*Jessi*? Her name is Jessica and she already has a boyfriend.'

'Yeah! I know that.'

'And do you know who her boyfriend is?' he asked. I shook my head.

'Well, it's Milind, our sales manager.'

'Milind? C'mon, he is old enough to be her Dad.'

'So, you don't believe me. I'll give the proof,' he dialled a number from his cell. 'See, its Mahesh's number and it is busy because Jessica is talking to him.'

'Please, why don't you leave me out of this? I don't care about it anyway. Mind your own business,' I said and left.

It was a Sunday, no office but no rest either. I was shifting to the flat again and that too with Paramjeet. I couldn't believe I was ready to do so. I prepared myself mentally and physically. I decided to join a Gym soon and till the time I kept a hockey stick for emergency. I was determined that this time if he provoked, I wouldn't spare him anymore, whatever may be the consequences later. I had decided.

'C'mon asshole! I owe you the scar on my forehead which changed my life forever. It was you who called me *Mamma's boy* for the first time. How can I ever forget that?' I charged myself within, seeing him.

'Hi! Somu, what's up?' he greeted.

'My name is Samarth,' I said with a fake smile but inside I was intending to break the stick on his head there itself.

I shut the door on his face. The room was empty for a long time and had turned dusty and dirty. First, cleaning and then settling my whole stuff in that 180 sq ft area all alone was something I was not expecting to do on my only off day for the week. Amey and Amar well acquainted with my laziness had already excused themselves for the day. Asking for help from Paramjeet was completely out of question and so I decided to dust the room myself and picked up the broom ... nothing is impossible for Sam, I encouraged myself.

Though it was not impossible, the task left me exhausted and tired. I was sweating like a pig and taking a shower seemed a great idea. But I didn't have the energy to walk to the bathroom and run the shower! I lay on my bed looking at the ceiling fan rotating; I tried to concentrate on each single blade to separate it from others, all against my persistence of vision law and realised some things in the world are really not possible for Sam. The exercise tired me further and soon I fell asleep.

I was not sure about the time but it had become dark outside. I had indeed, slept for a long time and was still not ready to leave the bed but somebody was at the door and knocking hard. I rose to check.

'Good evening,' it was Paramjeet. 'Hey! I made some coffee.'

'So ... what should I do?' I said and he looked clueless. I shut the door on his face.

I was feeling hungry and thought of Mom and home. Oh! How much I missed them! Now, I had to walk at least a mile to have some stale and pale *dal-chawal*. I really missed Pondy and especially my Mom. There are some real pros and cons living away from home but there was no use thinking on that terms, I had to take the pain to reach the mess anyway before closing time or would have to starve and regret later. But before that I needed a bath desperately because I was stinking badly.

※

After dinner, I lay again on my bed for my final innings of sleep but the noon's nap was too long to keep me turning and twisting over for more than an hour. I looked at my door, the light rays were still peeping in, Paramjeet was still awake and hence I decided to give it a final try but then thought that it would only be wastage of another half an hour. At last, I made my mind to watch some movie despite Paramjeet's presence; after all I paid half of the rent, so had every right to do what I liked.

'Not able to sleep?' he asked.

'No. Going for a jog,' I said with attitude.

'Okay, then lock the door from outside. You see, the Batman is just to come,' he said excitedly and popped some popcorn in his mouth.

I stood silent for sometime thinking what to say or do. I looked at him; he was completely engrossed in the movie. He howled sharply and jumped elatedly as the Batman made a dramatic entry and grabbed the villain. I drew back my steps to my room again.

'Samarth ...' he called. 'You can join me *yaar*, if you want. I know you love Batman.'

'No. You're wrong again. I hate such movies. I am not a kid any more to like such films.'

'C'mon, Batman Begins is a great movie,' he urged. 'Okay, Mr Grown-up, come to see Katie Holmes then. She is looking hot as ever!' he chuckled.

I did go and sit with him, not to see Katie, of course. C'mon, the movie was a better option than wasting time and energy sitting idle and struggling on the bed thinking of sex.

'Batman movies are good but the Spiderman series are far better when it comes to stunts,' he said as Batman flew his car over the roof of a house trying to save some lady.

'See Jeet, I hardly care. It would be better if you pop some more popcorn and shut your mouth,' I replied. But then, there was some truth in his words too. In my childhood, I was just crazy about Batman. I had this biggest collection of stickers, cards and comics of Batman and knew about all his enemies and gadgets. I would never miss the Batman series and would religiously follow the Justice League on the Cartoon Network even during exams and that's when Ekta Kapoor made her entry into the television with her sucking and everlasting tales of family dramas, and that is when the control of the remote shifted from my hand to Mom's. Since then, I had not really seen much of Batman and was seriously enjoying the movie with all my heart; but was careful not to show my happiness to Paramjeet.

'Aah! He is useless. Spiderman might have done it in a far better way,' Paramjeet remarked.

'But Spiderman is not real.'

'So is Batman,' he snapped at me immediately. I knew we couldn't and would never think from the same perspective and stopped the argument; the movie was at its last leg and ended with a bang. I was really feeling grateful to Paramjeet for those sweet memories of my childhood and started to think, if Amey had been right in his judgement about him.

'Samarth, do you like Hockey?' he asked and I shook my head. 'No *Chak de India* for me, I have to go to office the next morning,' I shot back. It was already morning; so engrossed I was that I didn't realise the time at all!

'Then, why have you brought that hockey stick with you?' asked Paramjeet.

Corporate Culture

There was no doubt, it was a dream but I didn't want it to end at all and was perhaps revelling in the experience because it's not every day you see such dreams. It was just me and my sweetheart Jessi surrounded by hills ... in the rain, dancing around the trees and singing a melodious duet ... And the lightning struck, she ran towards me, all wet and I grabbed her in my arms ... We let us fall on the ground and we came down rolling and tumbling, still in each other's arms. I was on her and was feeling the warmth of her breath on my face ... I kissed on her cheeks and she turned away shyly. I though went ahead, reached for her rosy lips and kissed ... I felt her mouth over mine and wanted to feel it again. I brushed my finger over her silky hair and then her ravishing pretty face, her aesthetically big eyes always reminded me of a particular heroine ... Ah! I forget her name all the time, she made her debut with SRK and the tall lady is always in news more for her boyfriends than her work. I could even hear the song she featured in *'Aankhon mein teri ajab si'*. Hey! That's my ringtone too ... and I woke up instantly to take the call.

'Good morning, Sam!', it was Deepak.

'Yeah!' I grunted still in sleep.

'So, dreaming of our Deepika Padukone,' he said.

'What?' I was shocked at his spot on answer.

'I mean Jessica, of course.'

'C'mon, tell me what's the matter?'

'Just come to Penguin Apartments, Sector 18, Nerul. Come right now,' his tone getting a bit sterner as he ended.

'But why? I need to go to office.'

'Don't ask any questions just do what I say,' he ordered.

I don't understand why people around me are so cynical about my rest and peace. Just ignore! That's what I do in such situations, certainly sleep is far much dearer to me than ... can't even think, that much. But then something was really wrong, Deepak was very serious and I had to check out what the matter was.

'Good morning,' I greeted.

'Hello brother,' he said with a big grin on his face. I was a bit boggled by his pleasant expression which seemed quite different from what I expected.

'Come with me,' he took me to the backside of the building.

'What's the matter?'

'Wait a minute,' he excused himself, his eyes were constantly searching for someone.

'What is it, *yaar*? Why are we hiding here? Tell me,' I was getting both curious and nervous. You see, these days cities are not safe for men, too.

'Shut your mouth and give me some time,' he said and continued sneaking from behind the wall while I stood silent beside him and finally ...

'Hey! Look. That's the matter.'

I checked ... it was Jessi?

'So, we are here to see Jessica's home. C'mon, I am not that serious,' I was though not that disappointed as I conveyed to Deepak from my expression.

'Dumb ass, it's my house that is here.'

'So, you both are neighbours?'

'Nope. She stays in Santacruz,' he screamed in disgust and pointed at the gate. It was our Sales Manager, Milind entering the same building.

'What is he doing here?' I asked but I guess I already knew the answer. I looked at Deepak praying hard whatever hovering over my mind to go wrong. *'C'mon slap me and say, you dirty mind!'* was all I was expecting from him but he stood still with a point-blank expression.

'Why? Why did you give them your house,' I dragged him aggressively onto the wall.

'Dude, calm down!' he consoled. 'If not me then somebody else will, if not she then again options are open. It's not anybody's fault. The world is mean and you have to compromise to succeed. That is what corporate culture is all about.'

I stayed mum on his explanation. I was feeling strongly dejected and crestfallen. Did I really have feelings for Jessica or was it just that it was Milind, whom I hated. I kept wondering why Jessica had to do that. Was money that important that she was ready to go to any extent? What would her parents say if they come to know about this and what about Milind? He has a daughter as old as Jessica ... still he didn't have any shame? These questions kept haunting my mind ... though I knew I would never get answers for these.

'Don't feel bad about her. She is enjoying her time; pun intended! Deepak laughed aloud saying it and I gave him one of my furious looks.

'Okay sorry *baba*. Forget it. It's getting late; we need to go to office.'

'You go, I won't come today.'

'Why? For her?' He paused and glanced at my face, which was still pale.

'Don't tell me, you're going to sulk all day? Samarth, you're still a kid to understand all this.'

'Yeah, maybe you're right. Why should I sulk? It's her life after all. I'll go to office only if you promise that you'll not eat my brain for the rest of the day.'

But promises are meant to be broken at least in Deepak's case. The moment the bus *vroomed*, he started all over again.

'Hey! I am sorry.'

'See Deepak, I am not at all thinking about her. It's just you who's always reminding me of her,' I bawled at him.

'I am not talking about that. I wanted to apologise for the other day.'

'Which day?'

'Well, I am sorry to have called you *Mamma's boy*, the other day.'

'Why are you apologising to me now,' I inquired; his apology was really a surprise, it was something I was least expecting.

'Because you love your Mom very much.'

'No, I don't,' I turned away to the window.

A minute later, I glanced at him from the corner of my eye; he was still staring at me.

'What? I do love my Mom. So, what's the big deal in it?' I said.

'Well, it's a big deal at least for me because I don't have mine.'

'Hello. May I speak to Mrs Geeta Mehta,' I said.

'Yes, who's this?'

'Good morning Ma'am, this is agent Sam calling you from Secure Life ...' I started as per the script.

'Listen,' she interrupted, 'I just want to say to you three things before I hung up. Firstly, I am not interested. Secondly, don't you dare call me again and lastly; I am no more Mrs Mehta.'

That was my first call on job and I didn't want it to end like that.

'So, are you divorced Ma'am?' I know it was weird to ask such a question to a stranger but still I didn't want to give up that early.

'You're getting personal,' she said in a serious tone.

'Sorry Ma'am, but our company has some good plans for divorced (I bit my tongue) ... I mean single women. Don't you think the time has come that women should be completely independent?' I said in a bold tone. Sandhya Ma'am and others seemed foxed to what and to whom I was talking and she put the speaker of the phone on to get hold of the whole conversation.

'You are absolutely right? Sorry to say but all you men are bastards. What do men think of us? Women have the power to give birth to a new life. It's not just cooking food and raising babies. Stay at home and you will understand we are the one who nurture the future of the country. And that's not all, today we're out too, walking shoulder to shoulder with men and also handling all the responsibilities. We've reached the moon and they still think we are just good at bed ... (she paused) ... sorry ... I got a little carried away.'

'I understand ma'am. It's really difficult for independent women to live single ... I mean single women to live independently, so our company has made many plans which would not only insure your life but also see that your finance grows and that is what Secure Life is known for.'

'Sounds interesting, can you explain.'

'Yes ma'am, it is a ULIP plan, i.e ... (I forgot the full form, Sandhya Ma'am prompted. Others looked amazed at my confidence) It is Unit Linked Investment Plan,' I said and turned the pages of the booklet to give the details. 'The premiums which you're going to pay are directly invested on shares of profitable companies and your money grows as per the market.'

'See, I am like completely alien to stocks. I just know that it's quite a risk these days and even the market is down.'

'I have a solution for that also. It's a matter of big money and investment, so terms and conditions can never be explained on phone. It's always better we sit and discuss on a one-on-one basis.'

'So, would you come to meet me? You seem to be quite interesting like your plan.'

'No, actually, we got an expert financial advisor who can clear all your doubts better. He can come to discuss these with you at a time suitable for you. You just have to tell when and where.'

'Okay, send him to my residence tomorrow after lunch. I would be free then and please try and send somebody as interesting like you,' her last line caught me completely offguard and did make me raise my eyebrows but my job was done—fix an appointment with the client. I got my first lead on my very first call and my whole team screamed hurray!

'What's that?' the call was still on.

'Nothing Ma'am, tomorrow our financial advisor will come to meet you after giving you a call,' I said and hung up.

I looked around, wow! I had gathered a good crowd around my table ... felt really great! The smile on everyone's face made me feel very proud. But Sandhya Ma'am didn't say anything ... she seemed a bit lost that day. There was something definitely wrong; else she was not the type to be so quiet. She looked rather disturbed, and her beautiful eyes seemed to convey nothing, it rather appeared clueless. And finally ...

'That was awesome!' Sandhya Ma'am complimented. 'Samarth, I appreciate your confidence level. Sky is the limit for you and I am highly impressed.' Though finally she said something; all was not okay ... I could sense that.

She had left her pen on my desk and I picked it up to return it to her. She was siiting in her cabin. I knocked and entered. She was holding her head and was resting on the chair. I was unable to see her face but definitely knew that she was sobbing. I reckoned I had landed at the wrong time. I had never seen her so upset. What was it? I wanted to know. But I had no right to ask, after all she was my boss and I couldn't dare ask her something personal. I still couldn't help myself and asked her anyway.

'Ma'am, is everything okay?' I blurted apprehensively.

'Oh, please! Not now, just leave me alone,' her voice was heavy.

'Well ... okay, I came to return your pen ... but before I leave, I'll advise you not to frown because you see, it takes seventy-two muscles to frown and just fourteen muscles to smile. And, I'll give you every reason to smile.'

'What ...? Who told you that?' she said, finally coming out of her siege.

'Well, I read it in a card which Shruti had given me once.'

'Shruti?' she asked in amazement.

'Yeah! My ex-girlfriend,' I replied.

'Wow! You had a girlfriend, that's interesting,' she laughed. The expression on her face was so different yet authentic. She was smiling because she really wanted to. But then, what was there to mock at.

'Hey! What's so funny in that? Can't I have a girlfriend?'

'No, nothing like that, you said *na* ... you'll give me every reason to smile and I think you indeed gave me one reason to smile.'

'Oh! That was no reason. What do you people think of me?'

'Okay, I totally believe you. Anyway, tell me, did you love her?'

'No actually ... eh ... she loved me.'

'Yeah Samarth, you're very sweet. Stay always the same. God bless you.'

The Birthday Girl

Things between me and Paramjeet were slowly getting normal. I can say that because we were watching a third cartoon film in a row and I was still not screaming. I looked at my watch, another fifteen minutes to go for the midnight and the mental torture continued. I failed to understand what was wrong with him, he had all these dialogues by heart, only God knows how many times he watched the same movies again and again and still he was always delighted about them. Anyways, thank you very much though for keeping me awake, no matter it was no less than a torment for me!

'Just wait for another month, its sequel would be out too,' he said.

'So what?' I gave him a dirty look, and lost my patience at last.

'It's Madagascar. It is a big hit.'

'Madagascar, Africa or Amazon I don't care. How could you tolerate a dancing and singing Lion, a giraffe having crush on a hippo and penguins who hijack ships? It's really disgusting and horrible,' I reacted.

'Oh! C'mon, it's just a cartoon film.'

'That's my point. Grow up kid, stop watching such movies. We are in college now, behave like grown-ups at least now,' I wanted him to understand the fact but knew it was of no use. He turned away angrily.

My phone was buzzing, it was already 12 a.m. It was Sandhya Ma'am's birthday. I was though in double mind to call her, after all she is a lady and married too, but most importantly she was my boss. Yet I think when it came to her, I hardly ever bothered about these formalities and dialled her number.

She didn't pick up the call and I was thinking whether or not to call her up again; so I kept trying until she finally answered on my fourth attempt!

'Hello,' it was a male voice. I reckoned it being her husband.

'Hello. Good evening sir.'

'Evening? It's midnight, I guess.'

'Sorry for that, sir. Actually, I called to wish Sandhya Ma'am ... it's her birthday I guess.'

'But she is sleeping and I don't think I will wake her up for you.'

'No problem, sir. I will wish her in office. Good night then.'

'Okay but remember, next time you call just check the time,' his simple advice meant much and I realised my mistake.

'Sorry sir, I just wanted to wish her ...' I tried to explain but he hung up. I was regretting and was deeply embarrassed.

∞

You cannot have a worse day than that. It's like you're taking a shower and have soap all over your body ... when you realise that there is no water ... only if you had taken pains to fill up the tank last night ... you curse yourself for being lazy. Then, you prefer walking to the station instead of an auto and miss the train, you regret for being a miser. Lastly, you're in the lift, with a beautiful woman who is all upset on her birthday just because of your stupidity ... how is one supposed to react in such a situation ... I didn't have any answer for it!

The door closed automatically and both of us waited for the other to press the button. She was standing closer to the button panel, all the same I reached my hand for the 7th floor, she too did the same and our hands lightly touched each other. Quickly, I drew back my hand. All I wanted was the lift to reach as soon as possible and just wanted to run away from her. But as I said the day was bad ... a power failure and the lift was stuck midway, just seconds before its destination. C'mon, what luck ... I thought. The office building was in the commercial hub of Vashi and they say the chances of power cut are almost nil! Why ... God ... why? There were many such occasions earlier wherein I had prayed for something like this to happen ... but not today. And now, when those 15 secs in it were unbearable, the lift got locked. How unfair was that?

From inside I was already in a panic situation but didn't want to show. I tried silly things like looking into my bag pretending to search for something, tried calling on phone, etc., to skip her glance. Yet, after a minute or so, there was nobody I could hear trying to help us out. Bloody lazy Security Guards!

'Are you always that stupid or is it a special day?' she finally broke the prolonged silence between us. I just returned a sheepish smile.

'Don't panic, *baba*, I won't rape you. Trust me,' she joked.

'No ... no ... it's nothing like that,' I said coldly.

'So ... you called me last night.'

'Yeah, you were sleeping. Sorry for calling you late. I wanted to be the first to wish you,' I said looking at the ground.

'I was awake when you had called,' she said, rather point blank. I was boggled by her answer but didn't dare to look up. Silence sunk in, again.

'Hey! Are you not going to wish me then?'

'Oh yes! Happy birthday Ma'am,' I wished.

'Thank you very much, but where is my gift,' she demanded like a child.

'Well, I didn't bring it. I thought you would be angry after last night.'

'Why should I be? I appreciate that somebody remembered my birthday at least. Thank you again and tell me what made you feel like that?'

'Don't know. But you seemed so upset today.'

'That's definitely not because of you ...' her voice fainted slowly and again there was a silence. She was definitely upset about something but then I guess it was not the right time to ask.

Few minutes later, the Guards still didn't bother to rescue us. But this time God showed some mercy on me and the power returned at last. The door opened and I gulped in a lungful of air, I was feeling suffocated inside the lift. But Sandhya Ma'am stepped outside the lift as if nothing had happened at all and the guards outside the lift stood up to salute. Asshole lazy jerks!

As I entered the training room, I realised Sandhya Ma'am was absolutely wrong. There were a lot of people who cared for her. And why not? Half of the office had a crush on her but she was ours ... I mean she was our boss, our team member and we had every right to celebrate her birthday.

'Hey! You didn't tell me about it,' I shouted at my team for keeping me away from it.

'C'mon, it's okay *yaar*. Now, shed some fifty bucks for the cake,' Rakesh said.

'No way, I am not paying.'

'That's why we didn't tell you.'

'Everybody just be ready. She is coming,' Deepak shouted from the door.

It was our office, so no carousing. It was just a cake with some candles and a small gift, no other props fluttering. But for Sandhya Ma'am, the world had stopped turning. She seemed deeply pleased by our efforts; she had tears in her eyes. She blew the candles and we clapped and cheered for her to blow all of them in a single breath. She cut the cake and we all hummed the birthday song. And, the first bite of the cake was, of course, for me; I was her favourite. Everybody else out there was feeling jealous!

'Well, thanks for all these; I owe a treat to you all. Anyway, I have two major news to share with you—one bad and the other good. The bad news is that today is the last day of your training session. From tomorrow you're going to be on floor with your headphones on, doing some business for the company,' she announced and we all booed.

'And, the good news is that I will give the treat which I owe today itself,' she declared and we all cheered in joy.

She took us to Golden Punjab for lunch. Cool place but very quiet! (Boring in other words) Quite different from my hangouts, I mean the prices were ten times higher and the quantity being equally low. (I don't want to comment on quality.) Yet, we were all free to order independently, after all she is well looked after by the company! Considering the eight of us (Sandhya Ma'am hardly eats), all willing to experiment and fill up too; the order was big. So, to kill time we played Truth and Dare.

The empty Coke bottle rolled and pointed towards Sandhya Ma'am. I was sitting in front of her, so I was to ask her a question.

'Truth or Dare.'

'Truth,' she said. I didn't have to think of the question, from the day one I had wanted to know this.

'Did you've a love marriage or an arranged one?' I asked.

'It was an arranged one. I had never met my husband before our engagement,' she said and I was like completely taken aback a little. I had not expected this answer from her. I mean ... she is no less than a hottie ... how could she go in for an arranged marriage, I thought.

'Ma'am, didn't you ever have a boyfriend?'

'I am just bound to answer one question of yours, and which I have already done.'

The rules say she was right and I couldn't argue. Mayur rolled the bottle again; it made a few revolutions and stopped exactly at 180 degrees from its previous position, on me!

'Truth or Dare,' she asked.

'Truth,' I said. It's always a better and safe choice considering the fact who the hell knows that you're not lying.

'Ma'am, can I ask him a question on your behalf,' Masood piped in.

'Hey! That's against the rule. Only Sandhya Ma'am is allowed to question me as per the rules,' I protested immediately.

This guy Masood was the youngest of us all, had just passed his 12th; yet he was the most cunning and mean amongst us. I always had a difference with him on everything. On my hit-list, he came second after Paramjeet.

'The question seems to be an interesting one, you seem to be very desperate. Whisper in my ears and I'll ask him the question,' she said and he whispered something while I waited for the question with bated breath.

She smiled hearing the question and took a deep breath. I almost skipped a heart beat seeing her actions. I wondered what the question was.

'Well, tell me ... Do you've a crush on me?' she asked.

What kind of question was that? She should kick him out of the job for this. I mean, she was our boss. Was it a way to behave like that? No matter however frank she appeared to be, one should stay in his limits and not take advantage of the situation, I thought. But that day, she was out of her mind, perhaps she had also become as crazy as us. She demanded her answer again and I remained all blank.

'C'mon, you have to answer,' everybody chimed in.

All I needed to say was just one 'no' but somehow I couldn't bring myself to utter it. I was thwarted and my heart was already sprinting at its best. Maybe, I was wrong, I thought; lying was really not easy and trust me, I couldn't.

'I like you very much and respect you a lot. Everybody does that. You're very good as a person and probably the most beautiful boss on earth ...'

'Yes or no, is what I want to hear,' she interrupted me.

'Yes,' I blurted.

She didn't look shocked or surprised but started laughing with others. I was feeling embarrassed but calmed myself, the game was still on. Masood would be questioned too. But then, the bad day was still on, nothing good could happen that day ... at least for me. The game stopped as three waiters lined up carrying our ordered cuisines. What the F ..., I thought and deliberately marked bad service in the customer's feedback slip after the lunch.

Our training was complete but before we took on our jobs, we had to pass a test. It was not a big deal though, these tests were always simple. Perhaps, it was not even of my standards. I mean, being an engineering student, I was versed till calculus of mathematics and then solving percentage related problems meant nothing to me. And, the theory part was more like standard seventh class English paper and that too of Marathi medium. Yet, my teammates were happily cheating!

When the results were declared, I had topped not only in the test but also was well ahead of everyone else in all respects. I got the best trainee award. Sandhya Ma'am presented me with a trophy and a gift coupon. I was really overwhelmed to receive it because the last time I won a prize was when I was in 4th grade for some G.K. quiz (seriously).

'Hey! What happened to you now?' I asked Deepak in the cafeteria. He appeared bleak and cold throughout the day.

'Nothing,' he shrugged but I knew something was bothering him. What was it?

'See, I hope it has got nothing to do with Sandhya Ma'am.'

'*Na re*, I'm thinking of something else.'

'What?'

'Will tell you later ... anyway congrats.'

'For what?'

'Best trainee award!'

'Not a big deal buddy,' I tried to be humble and generous in front of him. But it was indeed a big deal for me, after all it tagged me the best of the lot. I was happy to see him disappointed.

'I know what you're thinking,' he smiled. 'See, it's not because you've good communication skills or that you are very confident. It's not for your successful first call. It's because of that first bite of cake she gave you. It's because of the damn corporate culture.'

'What do you mean by that?'

'You know what I mean,' he said puckishly. I didn't argue further and stayed lull because I didn't want to show my emotions. But truly, what he said was no less than a blow for me!

'Don't mind it. I was just kidding.'

'Were you really? You see, there is always some truth behind every *'just kidding'*. Anyway, you're too practical to understand that.'

'Wow! That was too *filmy*. Well then, do you know why I was upset?' he said. I narrowed my eyes. 'But you promise you would take it easy (I nodded). I broke your i-pod.'

'What?' I grabbed it from his hand immediately; it was in two pieces, dead and gone. I was going mad ... crazy ... fuming ... how could he ... but he hardly cared.

'Sorry, it was just an accident. Chill *yaar*, you said you won't feel bad.'

'I said I would take it easy and that's why your head is still on your shoulders,' I hailed at him furiously.

'Phew! I am scared,' he laughed. 'Why do you worry so much man, when you are able to afford atleast ten of them.'

'And how is that?'

'C'mon, don't act so innocent,' he taunted again and I looked at him skeptically.

'Sam, it's Sandhya. Idiot! Forgot the corporate culture?'

'Stop it now!' I shouted at him. 'You've such a small mind. You're a real pimp.' But then, why was I reacting so violently—for me or for Sandhya Ma'am. Anyway, I couldn't be that mean. I respected her. However, it was from her side, that the positive vibes were coming from; at least Deepak thought that way and perhaps made me also think it that way. Truly, there are some real advantages of it and Sandhya Ma'am's company or whatever would be a real bonus. I was thinking mean but who cared? Unlike Jessica's case, we had just six years of difference and the fact that she was no less than a hottie; there was fun ahead. I smiled drawing all the conclusions in mind!

'If I'm a pimp then you're a bastard,' he read my mind again. And, we both had a hearty laugh over it.

'Hey! But what if you're completely wrong, I mean if she doesn't think that way then?'

'You know, I'm never wrong. Trust me. If I'm right then she is going to call you tonight. If she doesn't, I'll pay you for the i-pod.'

∽

From my very first salary, I bought a new i-pod because she did call that night. Seven months later, the world around me had changed completely ... not exactly ... or perhaps, it was just me who had changed. I was the call quality verifier while others were still telecallers; my salary was three times higher, free lunch and a cab to pick me up.

I had stopped being a puppet to Deepak; I hardly talked with him, not because of my higher status or something else but for the reason that other than that night's call, he was all wrong about Sandhya Ma'am. I don't understand emotions like Shalini nor could I read minds like Deepak's or evaluate on Amey's physical theorems, such equations had stopped existing for me long ago. Seven months of togetherness ... movies, dinners, shopping, night clubs, and long phone chats, yet I was not sure what it was? We hardly ever held hands ... not really, let me remember, maybe during those scary rides at the amusement parks, it was perhaps more than that and those small hugs at times, still no kiss, not even on the cheeks, where were we heading and what did she really want ... I never knew. I concluded, it was one of those inimitable relationships which are yet to be defined.

'So, you never really had a boyfriend ever?' I asked. We were out on our regular trips around the city. But she was no more new to Mumbai; we had almost explored each and every corner of the city in her Honda city. Perhaps, she had even known all the shortcuts to escape the toll booths.

That day perhaps at night, she parked the car near the sea-link between Bandra–Worli.

'Why do you always ask me that?'

'You don't seem to be someone who would go in for an arranged marriage.'

'To tell you the truth, I am not exactly the type who you perceive me to be. I was more like a tomboy in college.'

'Really?' I inquired. She was definitely lying, I thought.

'Hey! I am not lying,' she sounded a little agitated.

'Okay,' I said sheepishly. 'Tell me something more about your tomboyish days then!'

'Well ... I am the only girl in my family, so my upbringing was more like that of a boy. In fact I was completely oblivious of the girl world! I hardly ever had a girl-friend; I always hung out with my elder brother and his friends. I really miss those days.'

'So, how and why this transformation now.'

'C'mon, I am married now. My in-laws will kill me if they see me in jeans or minis. I mean ... marriage for an Indian woman means even today full stop to all fun and freedom.'

'Okay,' I grunted coldly. I didn't ask her anything more because she always got upset thinking of it.

'That's it? Don't you want to know further?' She said it so innocently that it brought a smile on my face and she continued ...

'I wanted to tell you about this since longtime. There was this guy Dhruv, my brother's classmate. He was an average student and belonged to a low middle-class family. He was a complete geek. We teased him all the time but he never reacted. He was very good at heart and I think he was a little eccentric too. He used to present me with a poem written by him on me, every time he came to my place. Without crossing his limits, he made realise that I was beautiful. His words introduced me with the girl in me and I developed a soft corner for him in my heart. I don't know whether I was in love or not but his company always made me happy. So, I wanted to know what he felt for me. But he was very shy and never responded ...', she paused; something was going in her mind and she smiled, ruminating it.

'Didn't you ever ask him about it?' I asked and she shook her head, still engrossed in thoughts. She continued after another break.

'Do you know something, Samarth? You resemble Dhruv so much, I mean the way you talk, move and all those funny things you do. That's why, we get along so well!'

'So, you think I am a geek,' I interrupted.

'Hey! It's not like that. He was clean from heart ... so are you and most importantly, I see the same respect for me in your eyes too, that I used to see in his. Even he used to be the first to call me on my birthday and now, I don't even know where he is. Actually, we lost touch after my marriage.'

'Not a big deal! If he's like me then definitely, he must be on Orkut or some other popular social network. Search him there. He would be really happy to know that you're happy in your new life.'

The smile which was on her face throughout the evening, disappeared at my comment. I realised I hit at her sore yet again—her marriage and her husband and like each time, the same silence sunk in.

'I hate this happily married tag.'

'I am sorry,' I said.

'Why are you feeling sorry Samarth? You know nothing about it. It's really not that good to have perfect life. I know it because I had one and believe me, it's horrible. My parents chose Aayush for me. He is good looking, well educated and rich—the perfect husband material. I was very happy to be married to him. But then, I realised that everything wasn't so good about him in our honeymoon itself. Making money, expanding business, foreign trips, buying comforts is what life meant for him and I was just a trophy wife for him. Love for him meant just sex and marriage meant producing kids. He neither understood me nor ever tried to do so. I tried my best to compromise but things between us only worsened even more. Except for the fights or arguments, we hardly share a word leave aside emotions or feelings. Our marriage is almost on the verge of split. I desperately want a divorce now, I hate him,' she was in tears after that. I didn't know what to do or how to soothe her and so I let her be. She sobbed for some time and then we finally drove off.

Unlike other days, no byes, no take cares, no see you, nothing ... she dropped me near my building. I stood outside her car; staring at her while she accelerated away. I was still there, standing. I heard her car to brake followed by the reverse tone and she drove back to my building.

'What?' she buzzed me.

'What ...?'

'Why are you standing here?'

'Well, I just want to say ... that you don't worry, everything will be alright. Though God never listens to me, but I will still pray to him for you. You really deserve more than this.'

'Thank you, I love you very much,' she smiled at last.

The End and the Beginning

*'Na umra ki seema ho na janm ka ho bandhan
Jab pyar kare koi toh dekhe kevel mann ...'*

Our relationship was no more a secret ... perhaps it was never ... but off late my whole world revolved around Sandhya Ma'am. She had divorced her husband and stayed alone. Her loneliness had brought us more close to each other. She was the new sales manager of our department since Mahesh had retired.

On my surreal love tale, there were plenty of comments posted to me by the people around me.

Deepak: the Corporate Culture rocks
Amar: born lucky
Paramjeet: love is blind
Amey: just fuck and forget
Shalini: fuck you

'So, what do you think about it?' I asked.

'What?' Amey grunted.

'C'mon, you know what.'

'See Sam, I came here just to relax a bit not to listen to your bullshit.'

'And you?' I shifted to Amar.

'Well, there is a difference between love and crush. When you like a person and you know why you like the person then it's a crush but when you like a person and do not know why you like the person, it's love then. So, now you decide what it is?' It has to be a forwarded sms; Amar's brain is too primitive for all these thoughtful things.

'You're right Amar; I really don't find any reasons for my feelings for her,' I said.

'Really?' he gave me skeptical stare. 'Let's also hear Paramjeet's take on this. So, what do you have to say?'

'Can't say actually, my experience in all this is nil. I find it too difficult to fall in love because people won't accept me the way I am and I can't do the same either. It's like a mix and match scheme I have tried out all the combinations but I stand out unique.'

'Wow! That's something good to hear,' Amey screamed in surprise, after all it's not always that Paramjeet made such a sensible statement.

'Anyways, what's your favourite movie?' Amey asked Paramjeet. The question was a blot from blue; something really struck our psychologist.

'*Brokeback Mountain*,' he replied without thinking. Must be another cartoon film, I thought.

'Cool choice *yaar* ... Can you get some water for me? Please. I'm dying of thirst,' Amey passed the empty bottle to Paramjeet and he went inside to fetch another bottle.

'Guys! Paramjeet is a gay.' Amey whispered. We (Amar and me) gave him a blank look.

'Sam, God save you. Be alert,' he added.

∽

'Hey sweetheart, what's up?' it was a call from Sandya Ma'am. Such cheesy names always fascinated me.

'Come to my place. I have a big surprise for you.'

'I'll be there in five minutes.'

Considering the fact that her home was 30 km away and bullet trains were still a distant dream, it was impossible. But I still tried my best to reach her place as early as I could.

'Hey! Come in,' she opened the door.

The scene inside somewhat reminded me of Pondy-Cherry, in other words, it was a complete mess. Empty cupboard, clothes scattered, suitcases pulled down, and furniture moved, somebody was going out for sure.

'Are we going somewhere?'

'I am going ...'

She had a very different smile on her face, I had never seen her this happy for quite a long time. I waited anxiously for her to continue.

'Honey, it's enough now,' she shouted. It clearly indicated, it wasn't I ... well ... who was the *honey* then?

I looked behind, there was a tall, dark and visibly handsome guy, standing. He waved at me with a smile but I was all bleak, wondering what was going on.

'This is Dhruv,' Sandhya Ma'am introduced. 'You were right. I found him in Orkut. He still loves me ...'

'But you didn't say anything about it?' I interrupted. It really didn't take fraction of a second then to understand the situation.

'I wanted to surprise you. I knew you would be very happy for me.'

'Yeah! I am.'

Sometimes, it is really difficult to produce a fake smile, especially to someone who could read my mind so well. I don't know if she ever knew that I loved her.

That was the last time I saw her. She went to Dubai with Dhruv forever. Sometimes, I missed her dearly but I've realised that it's really not the presence of someone that brings meaning to life but it's the way that someone touches your heart which gives life a beautiful meaning and she had, touched mine in her own very special way. Things between us never changed. Our inimitable and undefined relationship is still on, through mails and chats ... *international calls* ... are extreme to NRIs also!

ペ

'Your exams are over, you've quit your job ... so I don't find any reason for you to not accompany me,' Mom bawled at me. It was not just another statement; it was a declaration which by no means I could disregard. So, I was visiting my hometown Berhampore in Bengal after almost five years.

A trip to Bengal had always haunted me during my school vacation. Though I was a Bengali by birth, hardly did I ever possess anything particular to Bongs be it the mannerisms, looks, behaviour or taste. I more perceived myself to be a Mumbaikar whose parents spoke Bangla. I spoke fluent Marathi and also Gujarati (courtesy Shamita), Malayalam (courtesy Shruti) and Punjabi (courtesy Sandhya Ma'am), but I always struggled with my mother tongue. Yeah! Shame on me!

But that's not all. Being the only child of my parents, I've grown in my own ambience of space and privacy, something which is a hyperbole in my native place. Our house there was always full with relatives ... uncles, aunties, brothers, sisters, cousins, nephews, nieces ... There are many of my age in the family but I felt myself like an alien among them. We didn't have anything in common, be it our thinking, dressing, liking, disliking ... not even by a hair's breadth were any of these common. So, I barely exchanged a word with them except for Shreya. I always got along well with her just because she is the sweetest cousin sister one could ever wish for. And I was just not the one who thought so perhaps she was the darling of everyone, that's why the occasion was that big and special; it was her wedding after all. So, it was just not about Mom, like everyone else in the family, I too could not skip her marriage.

The 36 hours journey by train from Mumbai to Kolkata was not as bad as the 5 hours drive from Kolkata to Berhampore, thanks to some great highways which had not been repaired since the British Raj. And the rest, I mean from the bus stop to my home was even worse. If anyone really wished to enjoy a roller coaster ride, one just needed to take a cycle-rickshaw to my home and save some 500 bucks. Perhaps, it's more of a risky adventure considering the fact that there are no seat belts in it!

Though my ancestral house was big enough to accommodate all my relatives, yet after such a tiring journey I was unable to find an empty room to doze off. Marriage was not just a ceremony; it was a prodigious festival where anyone and everyone was invited. Perhaps, in this case, half of the district was included. No doubt, the occasion was a big chaos and needed lot of proper management for the events to pass on smoothly. Men were given the departments of food, decorations, invitations, accommodations, travels, rituals, etc., to handle while women were handed with the Herculean responsibility of grooming themselves and going through all the excitement and preparations; at times it was hard to figure out who was getting married ... as to who was the bride!

∾

'I'm from New Mumbai.' I introduced myself to one of my Mama's colleague from office.

'Wow!' she screamed out of joy. I was a little perplexed at her reaction. I thought she had heard it wrong for New York ... I mean she sounded that excited!

'Well, it's Navi Mumbai actually,' I corrected.

'Yeah, that's cool! How is Shahrukh Khan?' she said, getting more excited and even more curious.

C'mon now, how would I know? He doesn't stay in my colony. Such dull questions really suck. I understand that there may not be a common topic between us to talk on but SRK was something I least expected. 'I bet I never been in a range of 100km of SRK', I returned her a dirty look.

But it was not just from her, everybody else to whom I was introduced were all equally charged up about Mumbai and inquired me about Sachin, Salman, Hrithik, Amitabh, Aishwarya, and Sania Mirza ...!!

'Hey! she doesn't stay in Mumbai,' I hailed at that guy.

'So?' he grunted.

'Why are you asking me about her?'

'As if you know about the rest of the stars ... You Mumbai people are so flaunty.'

Fuck you! My mind screamed. I had a stronge urge to slap him but it was my sister's marriage and I being a *ladkiwallah* I had to be generous to the *baraatis*, no matter even if they were total jerks. I hated Mom for bringing me here. I looked around and there was the little bride, in the midst of chaos, Shreya was the only one most composed with a charming smile throughout the evening. She was looking her best in the wedding wardrobe. I always thought that Bengali dress up very funnily for marriages but that day, I realised how wrong I had been. Thinking of her, my eyes filled with tears, that was to be her last day at her own home. She would be a wife to somebody whom she had met just twice before and will be a part of family, she is completely oblivious of. Yet, getting into the new life that will be full of responsibilities had triumphed over the nostalgic feeling of having to leave behind the place and people she grew up with, all the same she seemed very happy.

I sat beside her at the dais for some time. At least there, the limelight was not Mumbai and the film stars! I was happy to pass on the gifts and pose for the photographs. And, not to mention the view I had from the dais ... of all the beautiful girls at the wedding!

One by one, they all came. They smiled, congratulated, presented bouquets, posed for photos and went off. I desperately searched for my Mama, so that he could introduce me to some of those beautiful girls, after all it is not always that a handsome and decent guy from Mumbai comes to Berhampore! I felt proud of myself. But luck was not to be with me ... Mama sent my Mom instead.

Her eyes widened and soon narrowed, seeing my closeness to the girls and I stepped back instantly. I took a seat while Mom took the charge. Five minutes later, I was feeling like pulling my hair for having missed all the action on stage which wasn't even two feet away from my seat. I was once a part of all the melodrama ... the hugs, shake hands and little peck on the cheeks ... but now I was just a disappointed spectator courtesy my Mom. I rose to stroll around a bit but one furious stare from my Mom and I parked my butt to the seat again.

And then, I saw her. I didn't know her name at that moment but when I did, it changed my world all over. She was wearing a blue *lanchha,* contrary to her skirt; her top was short which exposed her slim figure, perhaps one of the best I had seen recently. A few inches of high heel meant that she was short. Her curly hair covered her bare back. She was dusky and her eyes shone bright. She donned a shining but small *bindi* and her lips were traced with a gentle lip gloss. She was just stunning and the dazzling smile on her face, hit my mind like a big red BEST bus.

However, it was not just me who was smitten by her, destruction was on counter land also. She occasionally gave me a stare while I was transfixed by her striking beauty. She hugged Shreya and whispered something in her ear. Shreya looked puzzled at her words and she glanced at me, smilingly. It was something on me, I was damn sure. But what? I wanted to know. However, Mom's presence restricted my intention.

My eyes searched her madly all over but she had just vanished like Cinderella! Yet within, I knew we would meet again and it was just another beginning. My mind was yet again calculating, was it a crush or love according to Amar's formula, I wondered.

ᐁ

I hate myself for this; my sister was going for ever, the atmosphere was of melancholy, everyone around were sobbing and what was I doing; thinking of that strange girl ... it was something really mean of me to do so at that point of time. I wanted to ask Shreya about that girl as she came to hug me. She wept in my arms, making my shirt wet with liquid flowing from both her eyes and nose. My God! The shirt was of Tommy Hilfiger, I felt like crying for it but something else was bothering me even more. Yeah! The same girl ... where was she?

'I want to ask you something,' I whispered in Shreya's ear. By that time she had pulled down my pocket and also rubbed her *mehendi* on my shirt.

She looked up at me. The expression was similar to the one in the last night when the strange girl had murmured something in her ears. So, did the strange girl also ask her the same thing, I wondered. Shreya was silent again, I stared at her and she smiled at me before getting in the car.

She was still hovering in my mind as I found myself completely lost in a stream of thoughts. Her name was all, I wanted to know. I was feeling restless and wanted to talk. There was no way that I could discuss it with my other cousins. So, I thought of watching television to divert my mind. But what did I want to watch? I scanned through all the channels twice and it was all DD Bangla, ETV Bangla, Zee Bangla, ATN Bangla, Akash Bangla, Sangeet Bangla and many more.

'Don't you get MTV or Channel V here? I asked one of my aunts.

'What? You watch MTV!' My aunt was shocked. It seemed as if I had asked for some XXX CD!

༄

I never thought twice to go for the reception at Shreya's in-law's place; no matter it included a journey of four hours on world's worst roadways. Maybe, I was too bored at home or I just wanted to see Shreya or I was desperate to know about her friend. But still, I was a bit apprehensive since Shreya was close to my Mom. You never know, girls could never hold a secret.

'Somu Dada, what were you asking me the other day?' Shreya asked me.

'Yeah! I wanted to know ...' I paused to see Mom around while Shreya waited for me to complete. 'How is Jiju?'

She blushed on my reply.

'Oh! He is very loving and caring. And anyways I've something to tell you.'

'Really? What?'

'Her name is URVASHI ROY', she said softly near my ear but her words echoed constantly. Wow! Cool name, I thought.

'Who's she?' I tried to act smart but Shreya was smarter.

'Okay, if you don't remember her then it's not worth discussing. Actually, I got a message for you.'

'What?'

'But you're not interested, *na*?' She said and I gave her a dirty look.

'She too wants to meet you,' she said. You see, as guys don't like their friends to gape on their sisters, the vice versa condition doesn't hold back.

'Really?' I was overjoyed. 'When?'

'Cool down! Don't think much, she already has a boyfriend,' she giggled.

'Really?' I asked and she nodded. 'Nothing much *re*, I just wanted to see her once more but when? Maybe you ...'

'No,' she replied.

The daddy's girl

'What's really going on?' I shouted at Shreya, seeing her giggling with the other ladies at home. She was back within a week from her in-laws. No hitch whatsoever there, actually she had come home to complete some rituals. 'When are we going to meet Urvashi?' I reminded her about the promise.

'Yeah, I remember but let me first get out of all these rituals and ceremonies. These rituals and traditions suck. I would die following them all my life. It's a bane to be born as a girl.'

'Really? Anyway how are your in-laws?'

'They're real time morons; they hardly give us our space.'

'What ... who?' I butt in.

'Wanna meet her, *na*?' she warned.

I gave a sheepish smile, scratching my head.

'Sorry.'

'That's better. Mind it, next time.'

'Anyway, what's the name of your HE?' I said and she gave me a furious look. 'Seriously, I don't know, you didn't send a card to me.'

She took a pen and wrote his name Tejas on her hand. I tell you, wives like Shreya would rather die but not say their husband's name as tradition has it. And she still abuses old customs.

'Somu Dada, do you know how to fight?'

'Why?'

'Because her boyfriend has a brown belt in Karate,' she giggled and we both had a hearty laugh at it.

'Anyways, tell me something about her. Was she in your class?'

'My class? She is still in High School.'

'What?' I was eyeing a school girl. My friends back in Mumbai would tease me to death if they come to know about this child abuse. Sam! Raise your standard a bit, I said to myself. Why the hell do I never seem to get a girl of my age, I wondered.

'We were together in the music class. I warn you, she may seem innocent and childish but in reality she is a lot more than that. She is a total slut,' she added.

'But I thought you were friends.'

'Yes, of course we are ... you won't understand.' It's something that only girls can make out of other girls, you boys will never be able to understand that.'

It wasn't just me who was eager to see her. There were hundreds of missed calls and messages inundated in Shreya's cell from Urvashi. Lastly, came the call ...

'Yeah! Coming *re* in ten minutes,' Shreya said and hung up. We were already on our way.

'She stays here!' I exclaimed.

Her house is the historical monument of our city. It's an old and ruined mansion situated on the banks of Ganga, surrounded by trees and creepers. In my childhood days whenever I passed through it, I always wondered who really dwells in. Grandma used to recall it as a monster house and scare us with all sorts of horror stories about it, even threaten us to put in there if we didn't finish our milk. Actually, it was once a flourished palace of the rulers of the territory which meant Urvashi was a royal progeny. Wow! A princess is interested in me, I rejoiced. Amey and Amar would definitely feel envious.

'Welcome Mrs Shreya,' Urvashi teased and gave Shreya a hug but for me it was just a smile. She seemed so different; I wondered whether she was the same girl. The girl standing in front at that very moment was authentic—short, weak and poor. Her hair was messy, no make-up and banal dress up, the other day she seemed to have forged herself in her bold dress, glamour and attitude. Yet, I had a feeling in my heart which said that I was completely smitten by her.

I was always a dork in front of girls, and all these days I was going mad to know something about her. On the other hand, she seemed to be completely oblivious of me as she talked to Shreya continously. If boys like me don't know how to break into conservation then girls like them don't know how to end it. One hour gone, I was still dumb and they continued their whispers followed by loud laughs.

'Hello,' a call at Shreya's cell. From her husband, I could guess it from her expression. A minute short but full of giggles and smiles, and the call ended.

'I got to go, it's getting late,' Shreya cried looking at her watch.
'Cool phone!' Urvashi snatched the cell from Shreya's hand.
'Yeah! He gifted it to me,' Shreya replied.
We moved out of her place and she came along to escort.
'Shreya, is your cousin dumb?' she said with a slick smile.
'*Na re*, he is just shy by nature,' Shreya blushed. And still I couldn't gather courage to utter a word even.

'Really?' she reached for my ears. 'It's not an end, dear,' she whispered. Shreya stared suspiciously at her.

All the way back home she continued looking at me that way, was expecting me to say what Urvashi said in my ears. But even I was not sure what she had said? Shreya could have easily cleared my doubt but I didn't want to tell her about it; Amey always says that sisters are very good at messing love stories.

'What did she say?' Shreya finally broke in.

'Who?' I tried to ignore and she fumed at me. 'Nothing, she said that I'm cute.'

'Really? Somu Dada, don't let yourself down, okay? She has a horrible history of guys in her life ...'

'Hey, it's nothing like that, dear. Trust me.'

'Yeah! I trust you but not her.'

∞

Dekha toh tujhe yaar dil mein baji guitar ... My cell was ringing and I jumped off my bed.

I checked in, an unknown number blinking on the display. These promotional calls would never let us sleep in peace! I cursed and cut the call. It came again, straight for the fourth time and I disconnected again. Now, promotion calls don't hit more than twice, after all I had worked in a call center to know it only too well. So I kind of knew who it was. Yet, I was unsure whether to answer or not, as it buzzed for the fifth consecutive time. 'Hello' I gave in finally.

'Oh! hi there! Sleeping?' a female on other side.

'Shalini?'

'No, who's she?'

I tried to recognise the voice, was it Sandhya Ma'am ... no.

'Urvashi?' I blurted.

'That's great! At least you remember me.'

'But how and why?'

'Well, I sneaked the number from Shreya's cell in the morning.' Now that's something smart, *I am impressed.*

'I called because I want to meet you,' she added.

What? I couldn't believe my ears; I pinched my hand and *aah! It hurts,* I was not dreaming.

'Hello ... are you there?' she buzzed me.

'Yeah! But where do we meet? I don't know any place around here.'

'Leave that to me. Come at the *Ghat*.'

Love was in the air in Bengal and everyone seemed to have been infected by it. Just stroll around the riverside in the evening and you would spot couples all around. Actually, having a girlfriend was really not a big deal; all of them seemed *desperate wannabes.* Moreover, raising one was not even heavy on the pocket. From restaurants to theatres, the charges were very cheap compared to the rates in cities. Gardens and parks provided free hangouts for couples. And, people here preferred cycles over other vehicles. So in all ways I found the place very economical.

As I was unaware of the hangouts in Bengal, I always let Urvashi decide the meeting place. I always waited for her at the *Ghat* and she would take me to some lovers' point from there, both of us on our respective cycles. I enjoyed cycling with her; it not only allowed us more time together but also helped me to shed some of the fat from my butt which had grown in size after relishing all the wedding cuisines. Moreover, I neither had a bike nor did I know how to ride one. My friends always teased me to be a loser for that.

On our first outing, we travelled till the extreme end of the town to reach a deserted Shiva temple. Other than the formal greetings, I never talked much to her. Occasionally, she would ask me something and I would answer her briefly. We sat on the bench, waiting for each other to initiate.

'Somu! Are you going to speak something?'

I always hated people calling me that. But somehow the name sounded very sweet from her voice and I wanted her to say it again.

'Somu! Somu!' she shouted.

'Shreya said that you're already hitched with someone, then why me?'

'So what? You are from Mumbai, I thought you would understand. Mistakes do happen in life, it's not good to be right always. Sometimes, mistakes make you learn so much which you wouldn't have learnt otherwise.'

'What's your age?'

'Sixteen,' she replied. But truly her boldness and attitude didn't seem to match with that of a sixteen-year-old.

'And do you know we had been together since two years,' she added. That meant from fourteen, at that age we still fought for candies forget about getting into a relationship. *C'mon now Shamita's case was a different one*!

'So, how far did you go in the relationship?' I knew I had pulled the wrong card but it was too late to regret.

She gave me a furious look and then smiled.

'Emotionally or physically?'

'Both?' I guess it was a dim-witted one I am such a loser, I thought of myself!

'Emotionally, he resides in my heart and physically, we kiss, quite occasionally,' she paused in disappointedly and continued again.

'I hate kissing. He took them forcibly. And the last time we indulged in it was on the day before Shreya's wedding.'

'I want to end it,' she broke in tears and leaped on my shoulders. My heart almost skipped a heart beat as I felt the warmth of her touch.

'Hey, it's okay!' I tried to console her.

'Somu, I always wanted a guy like you in my life.'

It was too early to give a positive reply to that, I preferred to stay quiet. She was still resting over my shoulders; I gradually drew my hands to hers and held it tightly. But her mobile interrupted our romance. I looked at it. Rakesh calling, it displayed. She excused herself and took a few steps ahead. I was peering at her constantly. She seemed happy, her expressions were similar to Shreya's, whenever she talked to Tejas *jiju*. I was confused and furious too.

'Let's go,' I said after she disconnected the call.

We weren't walking together. I had slowed down thinking on the possible certainties and uncertainties of our relation.

'Somu, leave me. Don't be naughty,' she cried out. But it wasn't me; her *duppatta* had got stuck in the bushes. I tried to pull it out and she looked behind. I knew I couldn't explain, seeing her naughty smile. She reached for me and collapsed in my arms. My heart was beating fast as we tightened our hug. She raised her face and kissed on my chin. I lowered my head a bit to kiss her.

'Not now,' she said putting her hand on my lips.

I thought, finally I was growing into a big time Casanova or she was really very stupid not to realise. Things between us seemed to be moving fast. But who cared anyway? At last, I had found my source of entertainment in Kolkata! Perhaps, there was no harm to go for it until nobody knows about it. You see, it's really hard to wait for the right person in your life, especially when the wrong ones are so sexy and wonderful. I was bidding my time and enjoyed it thoroughly.

'Somu Dada, you seemed to be in such a jolly mood today, where have you been all evening?' Shreya asked.

'I was just strolling along the riverside.'

'Really?' she doubted and in no time she got the hint.

'You were with Urvashi, right?'

'Naah! You are wrong,' I tried to deny her accusations.

'I know it dada; only she uses this perfume ... O God ... you hugged her too,' she said, sniffing my shirt.

'Dada, please stay away from that bitch.'

∞

I was not expecting this. It was early in the morning—8.30 a.m. (it was early enough for someone like me). After my repeated requests following few dire threats even, finally MTV was there on TV. I was still under my quilt, just sneaking my head out, and was enjoying the morning show 'Kick Ass' and suddenly she appeared from nowhere and said, 'What's up?' my mouth was wide open as I thought-'HOW, WHY, FROM WHERE'. I didn't know. I jumped off my bed in shock.

'Ewwwww!' she turned away. Actually, I had only underpants on me.

I hurriedly wrapped the quilt and looked at her sheepishly.

'Where is Shreya?' She inquired.

'She ... must be in her room, I will call.' I moved out to fetch my clothes. I didn't bother whose or what was I putting on, I just wore whatever came to my hand. So, I ended up wearing Grandpa's *kurta* and Mama's shorts!

'Looking sexy,' she cried out.

'Thank you'.

'Where is she?' she demanded again.

'Shreya is a bit busy ... I guess; any problem if I give you company?'

'No, not at all. But she was to leave today, so I came to see her off.'

'Really? Dear lady then, how come you landed in my room? Her room is on the ground floor, you know, *na*?'

She returned a mischievous smile. I advanced towards her, she had congealed. I pulled her towards me and again she was in my arms. I looked into her beautiful eyes, they didn't fear me anymore.

'Your father must've been a thief because he stole the stars from the sky and put them in your eyes,' I praised them but she pushed me aside.

'What happened, Daddy's girl? Felt bad about it?'

'Don't you dare call me that?' she warned and left my room.

'Hey! Wait, what's wrong?' I yelled but she didn't stop.

☙

I tried her number over a hundred times but she didn't respond. Finally she put off her cell. I didn't understand what really hurt her so much and the only way to find out was to ask Shreya. But then, she wouldn't also not tell me everything.

'Shreya, do you remember when I last helped you, out of a trouble.'

'Let me remember ... never ... perhaps you always created them,' she pointed at a burn mark on her arm, I happened to stick a hot rod there. I was just seven then.

'It was an accident, Shreya'.

'Really? Anyway, come to the point. I hope it's not related to Urvashi.'

'Ehh ... Yeah! It is!'

'She seemed very disturbed today. Did you try to rape her or what? No, in that case, she wouldn't have been upset.'

'C'mon now, I am serious.'

'Okay then, tell me what happened.'

I narrated everything to Shreya, uncensored.

'You asked her something you should never have, her Dad. You know *na*, her link with the royal family. (I nodded). Actually, her Dad ditched her Mom and married someone else in Kolkata. And her mother was just given the ruined palace in alimony. Raising herself and Urvashi had always been tough for her Mom. She works day and night to feed her family. Her Mom was never able to spend quality time with Urvashi and that's why she is like this. There was no one to advise her or make her understand. She feels it's only because of her Dad that they are suffering and hates him to the core,' Shreya narrated.

'That's very sad.'

'But we cannot do anything about it. So, it's always better that you stay off it, okay?'

∾

I have always known to be very sensitive. And Urvashi's background had made a deep impact on my mind; it had brought her all the more closer to me. There was a sudden change in my perception and intuition towards her. Though I was not sure whether it was love or mere sympathy. Anyhow, I had started caring for her and needed to tell her that.

Shreya returned to her husband and so did Mom too. I stayed back for some time, thanks to Grandma's testimonies. And I didn't waste any time after that, I followed Urvashi all day, everywhere (I mean wherever it was possible) she went but she never acknowledged my presence. However, I was desperate to speak to her and one day landed at her music class.

Getting in was never a problem, nevertheless I was the nephew of Mr Subir Moullik, a renowned CPI party leader. I strolled through the passage and got inside the auditorium. Considering the fact it was a classical music show, the number of people on stage were actually more than the people in the audience! Urvashi too was on the stage. Perhaps, on the mike, she was to sing and so, I took a seat.

She sang Gurudev Tagore's *'Ami Chini go Chini'*. No doubt, the song had to be magical and mesmerising though the lyrics were a complete bouncer for me. But being a music lover, I could still feel its essence. She completed and I clapped, until everyone stopped and stared at me. I followed Urvashi backstage.

'What is it now? Stop irritating me or else I'll shout,' she rebuked.

'I just want to let you know ... I know who you really are. And you're better than that.'

'What?'

'I'm sorry for that day. Please, forgive me. I'm ready to do anything for whatever happened.'

'Anything?'

I nodded, 'Yes'.

'Well then, sing a song for me on the stage.'

'But I don't know any Bengali song.'

'Okay, sing an English song then.'

Her reaction was so instant. It really made me to think, was it all planned?

'Don't feel scared, a lot of people have no talent at all, I understand. So, see you tomorrow at three,' she taunted. But pretty lady, what you don't know is that I was the Bryan Adams of my school, I thought and smiled.

Back at home, I was wondering what to sing. I really wanted it to be a special one and knew that any English song wouldn't make the impact I wished to create. It had to be something very special. I scratched each and every nerve of my brain and got an idea, perhaps a brilliant one. But I needed someone's help for its implementation, so without any hesitation I dialled my troubleshooter's number.

'Hello' Shreya picked up after a long ring and that also on my seventh attempt.

'What really made you answer the phone so late?'

'Damn! I'm on my honeymoon.'

'But you had said ...'

'That was just a dialogue,' she cut me off. 'What do you want now?'

I explained everything to her. She readily agreed to help on the condition that I would not disturb her for the next two weeks.

∞

And so, I was ready with my song and was waiting for Urvashi. She arrived with a gang of 6–7 girls following her. She had made full arrangement to embarrass me.

'I guess you know at least what it is?' she said pointing at my guitar.

'Just sit back and watch,' I said and marched for the stage.

I adjusted the leads with the keys. Urvashi and her friends still didn't have an idea what was to follow. And I began my song ...

I know you, I know you, I know you
Oh! my lady from a foreign land
You dwell in the land afar
Oh! my lady from the foreign land.

> *I saw you on an autumn dawn*
> *And again when night adorn*
> *I saw you in the depth of my heart*
> *Oh! fair lady from afar.*
>
> *I turn my ears to the sky*
> *And catch tunes of thy songs that fly*
> *I offer my soul to you*
> *Oh! fair one from afar.*
>
> *I travelled the land and sea*
> *And came to a land where I longed to be*
> *I am a visitor at your door step*
> *Oh! my fair lady from afar.*
>
> *I know you, I know you, I know you*
> *Oh! fair one from afar ...*

It was just the English translation of the song which Urvashi sang the previous day. My performance was at its best and the audience was spellbound. Why would not they be? Shreya had tried her best to preserve the grace of the great poet's words while translating and I had worked on it the whole night, to set the tunes on the six strings which I arranged from a friend.

I bowed after my performance at the audience who were enthusiastically lauding me. Urvashi came to meet me backstage.

'So, what do you have to say now?' I asked Urvashi.

'I love you, do you love me?' She proposed.

My first romance

I was confused searching for the right combination to wear; I was to meet Urvashi's Mom in the evening. No, nothing like that, it had been only a day after her proposal. Actually, she wanted to introduce me to her Mom, before moving ahead on a relationship with me. I finally, zeroed on a formal and simple get up; after all I didn't have to smitten her Mom.

'Hello ma'am,' I greeted at the woman who was checking on some files. I though, had a doubt for her being the lady awaited.

'Yes,' she looked at me through her thick bulletproof glasses.

'Urvashi?'

'I am her Mom,' she replied.

Well, comparing the dull lady with her hot daughter, I concluded that her husband had the major contribution in the making of their daughter, Urvashi. I also realised as to why her husband had deserted her.

'Well, I am Shreya's cousin. Actually, she needs Urvashi's music diary since she missed a few classes. So, I came to collect it.'

'Okay, I'll call her,' her voice was so dull that it made me think whether she suffered from some serious ailment.

'Urvashi ... Urvashi ...' she shouted but the sound waves generated could hardly reach Urvashi's ears.

'Well, she must be in her room. So, if you don't mind, please go and meet her there.'

And Ma'am why would I mind it, I thought to myself.

'Okay,' I said rather coldly.

'It's right from the passage,' she instructed.

Due to the financial constraints that part of the mansion was left unrepaired and unmodified. So, her room remained vintage and royal. As I entered her room, I thought I was peering through her Mom's specs. Everything around seemed to be magnified. The room was as big as our classroom and the other accessories and occupied furniture equally huge in size. The windows were larger than the door of my apartment! At the centre, was a gigantic bed, just inches short in dimension from our hostel room. And there was my little lady love resting on the huge bed, totally engrossed reading something. Might be Economics, I guessed. Twelfth exams were nearing!

'Boo!' I shocked her from behind and she trembled in fear, down fell her book. I picked it and what? What was she reading? A *Debonair* magazine! Now, that was something I had not expected. I was completely shocked.

'What's this?' I questioned.

'As if you don't know?'

'C'mon, how can you read this?'

'I am not that bad in English, dear?'

'Bad joke!'

'I agree that these things are common among you boys. I mean, we've also got some desires and fantasies,' she justified.

Her lines reminded of someone very close to me—Amey. Truly, she was the female version of my wild and horny friend, Amey. Maybe, that's why, I always got attracted towards her.

'So you met my Ma.'

I nodded. 'She only told me that you're here.'

'It seems that she liked you very much. Into the bedroom on the first day itself, good going!' she laughed.

'Really? Anyway, what's wrong with her? Why is she looking so pale and tired?'

'Ma works in a government firm. You know *na,* after some years of work there you become like that.'

'What?' I laughed.

'Hey! She is my Ma. Stop it and come with me.' She held my hand and led me to her Mom again.

'Mom, I guess both of you had a proper introduction,' she said.

'Yeah! He is Shreya's cousin.'

'Ma, Somu Dada is from Mumbai and very much fascinated to see our palace. Can I show him around our house?' she said.

'Dada'? Did I hear it right? I gave her furious look. She winked at me.

'It's no more the glorious palace it used to be some years ago. Her Mom broke into her emotional story.

'Ma, stop it. He's a stranger,' Urvashi interrupted.

Anyways, her *Tour de Palace* landed us on her terrace. It was dark, big and ruined. It had walls of chest high which prevented spying in. In one word it was a paradise for lovers. She glared at me for my take on that.

'Am I dead, angel? Because this must be heaven.'

'What? From where did you learn these filmy dialogues?'

'Girls love humorous guys ... I mean guys with good sense of humour.'

'Please, try to talk something sensible.'

'Really? Then what was happening downstairs? Am I your Dada?'

'Then what should I have said to Ma? Meet my boyfriend!' she got a little agitated.

Yeah! She had a point, so I kept quiet. But calling me Dada was weird I thought!

'Don't feel bad about it. It's okay here. Girls call every new guy Dada here; no matter later they turn out to be their boyfriend or even husband,' she clarified.

I smiled at her reply. Though being younger to me by five years, she still always talked more sensibly than me. More the time I spend with her, the more I got impressed by her bold nature.

'So, other than singing, what are your other hobbies?'

'Somu! she cried out. 'Are we here to discuss my hobbies?'

'Then?'

'Idiot! Look around this place, even if you make me naked, nobody would come to know.'

'So? I really didn't have an idea, what she was hinting at? Frankly speaking, I feared to be raped again.

'So ... so what? Do I have to invite you to kiss me?'

I heaved a sigh of relief. I glanced at her, her eyes looked naughty and her lips enamoured me, I kissed ... I mean, we kissed but it was just a kiss, not a smooch.

'Girlie, you're such a bad kisser,' I stated.

'Really? But you seem to be an expert. Till now, how many of them have you gone with?'

'C'mon, you're my first girlfriend and this was my first kiss,' I lied because somehow, a girl's heart cannot bear a truth. They know that we are lying, yet are happy with it.

'I can't believe you on that ... Anyway, the reason we are here for.'

I looked at her suspiciously, she scared with something unaccepted everytime and so I was waiting for the next surprise with bated breath. She took me at the backside edge of the terrace; a part of barrier had tumbled down and there was wide gap. She still moved ahead till the dead end and I had to follow. I grasped her tightly, not because of any romantic or erotic feeling but I have a dreadful fear of heights.

'Can you see that tower, there?' she pointed at the tower, perhaps half of it had already toppled a long time ago. It was merely some fifteen feet away from where we were standing.

I nodded.

'Come there at seven tomorrow and wait for me. The gate is broken, you won't have any problem. And come with a torch and a stick,' she added. I wondered what she really meant. Were we to tear into someone's house or dig an ancient treasure or simply go for sex? With her possibilities were always endless.

'A torch and a stick?'

'Well, it's rumoured that my great-grandfather's spirit is haunting that place.'

'What?'

'Kidding dear, anyway it's getting late. Ma would suspect, let's move.'

I bid her Ma bye and Urvashi came with me to drop me at the gate.

'Well then, bye' I said.

'Just bye ... don't you want a good-bye kiss. You are so unromantic!' she said with a mischievous smile, I grinned too. She pulled me to a dark corner; I held her in my arms and kissed her on the cheeks. And then, advanced for her lips.

'Wait a minute ... Control your tongue this time.'

I got reminder messages, missed calls and calls from Urvashi all day. I had switched to a local number and so it really didn't matter. And at exactly seven I was climbing the deadly tower. I regretted not bringing a torch along. Though I was not sure that the structure could withstand my weight yet somehow holding on the walls, I managed to reach the top. I called her.

'I've reached,' I said.

'I can see,' she replied. I looked around; she was at her terrace, waving her hand at me.

'So, what next?'

'Well, can you see that bridge there? Just walk on that and come to me.'

'Bridge? It's a mere wooden plank, are you crazy? I can fall and die.'

'Don't worry, nothing will happen, it's strong enough.'

'But I fear heights.'

'You love me *na*?'

'Yes.'

'Then come.' She hung up. I don't know what was on my mind exactly but something forced me to go against the odds and I walked towards the bridge.

'Are you scared?' she asked. I had reached halfway, still far enough for her whispers to be audible.

'Don't distract me?' I yelled. But she got it the other way and that also completely wrong, she walked in my way from the other side. I froze in terror, don't panic! I said to myself. When my testicles contracted between my thighs out of dread, she eased out casually as if walking on a ramp.

'This is for our love' she pecked my cheeks. I was sure, she wouldn't have minded for a one on lips either but then getting off the edge safely was all that was on my head at that time. And finally, after a few hiccups and thousands of my baby steps, I reached to safety.

'Wow! That was awesome!' She exclaimed. I nodded with a smile but from inside my bones were still shaking.

'Are you going to love me that much, all through life?'

'Yeah! Of course,' I replied and she kissed on my lips.

'Somu, I've always dreamt of having a big bungalow on a beach. Promise me you would get me one!' Her eyes demanded a yes and I had to nod. That's really the magic of love; you don't get irritated with such rubbish thoughts. First, my graduation was on stack, I was not sure how I would buy our bread for living and secondly, did she even have an idea of the prices of land in Mumbai? Foolish girl! It is so hard to explain real stuff to girls; they could never understand the reality. They are better in their dream world and for me, it was better to join her with crap stuff.

'Why not? I promise'. And sweetie, we'll have half a dozen kids, so that you never feel lonely,' I cuddled around her neck.

'Excuse me!' she pushed me aside. 'You're so mean and selfish. Do you know how painful it is to give birth to a baby? You just want to screw me day and night for your lust. I hate you.'

'Sorry, I didn't mean that.'

'You should be,' she almost sobbed.

'Okay, forget it. Tell me how you managed to put that plank there,' I tried to drift her mind.

'Well! That's a secret and I don't trust you to tell you that.'

'If it was a joke then it wasn't funny at all. Now tell me, how?'

'I am serious,' she hailed at me furiously.

'It was scary, anyway.'

'Really? Then, be used to it because you would have to come this way only, if you wish to see me daily.'

'But why?' My mouth wide opened.

'I got my school in the morning, music class in the noon and tuitions in the evening. So, no slot for love in the day and at night Ma won't allow me out and perhaps, this is only safe place wherein we can meet.'

'Safe?'

'Oh! You're such a coward. Rakesh wouldn't have minded it at all.'

'Who's he?'

'My beau.'

To that extent a girl can kill your self-respect and honour; you never feel bad on any of such hardcore insults. Sometimes, they are really mean but you still love them and so did I. Actually, there was something I fear more than the height, her grandfather's spirit and my Mom. I feared being away from her, the most and so I always agreed to whatever she demanded. It was just a couple of days of love and I was already feeling the magic of it or better say the curse. I was getting enamoured, being close, being loved and being possessed.

∾

'I already told you about it but I never believed but today I saw you and him together. Damn! Urvashi, you said you love me,' I bawled at her.

'I do but then it's just been a week with you. He is in my life since two years and I cannot ignore that fact. I need some time.'

'I risk my life every day, just to meet and you play games behind my back. It's over now. Go to hell.'

'Well, if you really want me to go there, then definitely I will' she hung up furiously.

Her mind was just out of this world, I knew she fears nothing and can do anything to impose her will. She was that stubborn! I cursed myself in despair and called her but her cell was already switched off. And so, I rushed to her place.

There was a strange silence over there. It was noon; her Mom was out for work. As I realised she was all alone, my heart started beating faster. I advanced towards her room steadily and anxiously. I sneaked into her room, my heart had almost come to my mouth but finally I found her safe ... playing games on her mobile.

'But you were to go to hell, *na?*'

'Yeah! This game is real hell, but you see I don't have any other option in my cell,' she said casually as if nothing had happened. Girls can be unpredictable to that level!

'So, what brings you here?' she added with a very mischievous smile on her face.

'I'm leaving,' I shouted.

'Somu, wait! I need you,' she cried. 'See, I twisted my ankle in the morning and it's paining. Can you please help me apply Iodex?'

'Yeah! Sure.'

I held her bare leg in my hand. It was smooth and hairless contrary to my leg. I applied the black cream and massaged it a bit. I glanced at her; she had rested her head on the pillow, her mouth open and eyes closed as if I was ... her sedative gesture had at least aroused me; I stopped and rose to move. But she held my hand.

'Somu, come here. Love me,' she pulled me and in another second I was on top of her, kissing her.

And after twenty minutes of having sex ... no ... this time making love, I would say, we were peering into each other's eyes, lost in our own world of romance. She finally broke the momentum by getting into my arms again. I kissed her on her forehead; she looked at me and said.

'Do you now believe that I love you?'

Her statement put a question mark on my mind. Is sex an integral part of love? Is it the ultimate proof of commitment? At least for a guy like me, it's always been a mere fun but for girls like Urvashi, it meant much more than that, I realised it that day. And, this realisation put in a strong feeling of guilt within me, after all she was just sixteen, a school girl and I hadn't used a condom.

The Betrayal

'You gifted her a N-70,' Amar was shocked.

'So what? I love her very much. Guys, I am committed,' I said. I had just returned from Bengal and had called upon my friends to boast of my adventure there.

'Really', it was Amey.

My phone vibrated, a missed call from Urvashi which indicated that she was free and alone at home. I excused myself and went to the balcony to call her.

'Hello honey! Love you ... love you,' she started with her usual way of wishing.

'Yeah! Me too,' I shouted knowing very well that the three bastards had stuck their ears to my conversation with Urvashi.

'What's wrong with you, today?' she questioned.

'I am with my friends actually. Can I call you sometime later?'

'Is that how much you love me Somu, I hate you,' she bawled at me.

'Honey, listen!' But beep, beep, she disconnected the call. I returned, to the hall.

'What happened honey?' Amey teased.

'What? It's normal, people do fight in relationship. It's nothing new,' I tried to justify.

'Really?' said Amey sarcastically.

'I don't know but our relationship seems to be heading nowhere ever since I returned. Each time she finds some or the other reason to fight with me and we end up shouting at each other rather than talk. I am actually quite fed up with her reliability and loyalty tests. Can't she understand that I love her and that both of us don't need to justify anything to each other?'

'What makes you think that she loves you? Just because she slept with you, it does not mean that she should love you,' Amey said.

'Please, Amey! Mind your language,' I pleaded.

'Tell me, did you guys use protection.'

'Just fuck off, Amey!'

'What do you both think?' he asked Amar and Paramjeet. As usual, Amar could not think of anything and shrugged off while Paramjeet delivered yet another heavy dialogue.

'Sex is something that I'll never understand. Some think it's necessary and some think it's lousy. I rather choose not to think at all. After all, it seldom requires brain,' said Paramjeet.

'C'mon guys, I am serious,' I broke in.

'See Sam, stay away from all these. You are not yet ready for love and commitment. This is not the age and this not the end, just "fuck n forget". You have done it before also so just don't bother about all this, it is as simple as that!'

Somehow for the first time in my life Amey's advice didn't affect me at all, I distanced myself from him. Perhaps, with everyone who disapproved of my love story. Urvashi! Urvashi!

And Urvashi, I knew nothing more than that. I had lost interest in almost everything. No big dreams, no Grammies, no Red Chillies, nothing, I just wished for a steady life with Urvashi. I would spend my entire day just waiting for the time when I could call her. Undoubtedly, my mobile bills were going soaring heights in spite of all the cheap STD plans being activated and it was becoming really difficult to afford them with my minimal pocket money. So, I had to cut on almost everything that was dear to me ... pizzas, a first class pass, movies, and deodorants, even a plate of *vada-sambhar* at my college canteen had became luxury for me. On the other hand, I wondered if she too harboured same kind of feelings for me? Her demands and expectations had continued to fledge on, and arguments become even more regular. But still somehow, I just could not cut off from her; I just seemed to be drowning in the pool of false love.

ೞ

'Hey! What's up?' It was Shalini. 'How come you are in Rasayani?' After a long time she had visited my place.

'C'mon, it's my home dear!'

'Anyways, you seemed to be a bit disturbed. Anything wrong?'

'Yeah! I had a fight with my girlfriend.'

'Who, Sandhya?'

I shook my head.

'Then, Shruti?'

'No *re*, her name is Urvashi. You don't know her.'

'What? A new girl, it's really disgusting, Sam!' she screamed.

I wanted to talk about Urvashi and my relationship with her to Shalini so I confessed everything that had happened in Kolkata.

'Sam, I think you are moving too fast in this relationship. Be careful before it ends in a disaster. Don't make yourself her slave; you're a man after all.'

'Really? I mean ... is that what you feel the relation is heading towards ... I am becoming her slave?'

'What? Aren't you even realising it?'

'No, I mean thanks for the advise. I won't let her dominate my life anymore, I never realised it. I will sort out everything today itself.'

'Yeah! That's more like it Somu, my dear friend.'

'See, I forgot to ask you, tell me, what will you have?'

'Oh! please, don't bother about all this, I just came to meet you.'

'C'mon, have some coffee at least.'

'Okay, if you insist!'

In Mom's absence there are not many options at my place. My skills in kitchen is limited to just boiling water and adding coffee, milk powder and sugar to it, not a big deal. No matter, how bad I may be, Shalini would still appreciate it. After all, she is my best friend. So, I was back in ten minutes with two cups of coffee and some biscuits.

'I am Shalini, his friend,' Shalini said answering my phone, 'Wait a sec ... here he is ... Sam, your call,' Shalini handed the phone to me.

'Who's it?' I asked her.

'Don't know, somebody called US.'

Oh! My God I am dead. US stood for Urvashi and Samarth. Urvashi talked with Shalini, meant it was death knell for me now.

'Hi! Honey, what's up?' I said.

'So, in Mumbai, you have another girlfriend? You're a playboy. I hate you ... I hate you,' she shouted and disconnected the call. Of late, she used the *hate* word more than *love*.

'Sorry, actually I didn't realise,' Shalini said guiltily.

'It's okay! I'll convince her. Anyway, tell me about you? How's your beau?'

'Well,' she inhaled a gallon of air, which meant something was wrong. 'We broke up,' (I was right. I had started to understand girls very well. Damn! I didn't quite appreciate it.)

'Why?'

'Oh! don't ask me about it? It's a painful episode of my life, I don't want to discuss it.'

'Yeah! I understand.'

'Hey! C'mon, now watching him walk out of my life does not make me bitter or cynical about love. But rather makes me realise that if I wanted so much to be with the wrong person how beautiful it will be when the right one comes along.'

It's really very easy to say something like that but emotions can never be hidden. I gave her a *jadu ki jhappi* to comfort her.

'Somu! What's happening here?' I don't know from where the hell, Mom landed there all of sudden.

∾

'Char dino ka pyar oh rabba, lambi judai lambi judai.' The song somehow reminded me of my own love story, its lyrics perfectly suited my romance with Urvashi.

I smiled recalling those lovely moments of my life. I love her and damn with everything else, I said to myself. I was missing her terribly and so I dialled her number. She disconnected my call several times, there were still three hours to go before our official calling time started. But I couldn't wait any longer. I just wanted to listen to her sweet voice once; just a hello would have been enough. So, I called her from my Dad's cell, again she cut twice but on my third attempt, I was lucky.

'Who's it?' she said rather irritated.
'Guess, sweetheart!' I said.
'Somu!' she shrieked.
'What is it, honey?' I heard a voice from the background.
'Urvashi, who's there with you?' I oppugned.
'Eh ... eh ... I will call you later,' she hung up. I tried her number again. But her phone was switched off.

Who was he? I wondered. Rakesh! Or, maybe someone else, you never know. She is so unpredictable. I hate her, I said to myself but yet I was waiting desperately waiting for her call. Those hours seemed to be the longest hours of my life. And finally, after two hours my phone was ringing.

'Hello!' she said.
'So ... do you've an explanation?' I was rude to her for the first time.
'What do you mean by that? When you can move around with other girls in Mumbai, I am free too Somu. Anyway, who're you to ask me for an explanation?'
'Who am I? You ask yourself! Damn Urvashi! I seriously love you.'
'Really, then marry me.'
'What? Have you gone crazy?'
'Why? You said *na*, you love me.'
'Urvashi, I mean you're just sixteen and I'm nineteen ...'
'Twenty.'
'Yeah, whatever, we are too young to get married. I love you very much. Just wait for a few years, we will definitely be together.'
'So, is there no age bar for sex? I mean ... why didn't you think of it at that time?'
'It was you who wanted to do it.'

'What? This is what you think of me. I hate you ... I hate you ...'

'I didn't mean it.'

'Go to hell now.' She hung up and switched off her cell.

I cursed myself in anguish for hurting her but I had to wait another sleepless night thinking of her. C'mon Sam, get over it, I scolded myself.

∽

It might be that I was very tired after a hectic day in college or was it mere boredom ... I don't know ... but that night I managed to sleep peacefully at last. I was actually, lying on the sofa browsing through the newspaper and I didn't even realise when I soothed to snooze. But my phone buzzed me off, I was not sure of the time but it was near to dawn, I reckoned since I couldn't hear Mom moving around.

'Hello,' I said, still sleepy. It was an unknown number.

'Somu!'

'Urvashi!' I exclaimed and jumped off my cozy couch. 'I am sorry for last night. I didn't mean it. Please, sweetie, forgive me. I love you very much.'

But there was no reply from her side.

'Urvashi! Urvashi! Please, say something, don't do this to me ...' I pleaded.

'Calm down, Somu! Listen to me carefully, I am sorry but I had to do it.' She stopped in between and I was anxiously waiting for her to complete.

'Just tell him, okay!' Somebody was prompting at her back. I guessed I knew him, perhaps I had an idea of what was happening out there and I was very angry at her, but I wanted my instincts to go wrong this time. But then truth is what matters in the end, whether you care about it or not.

'Somu ... I eloped with Rakesh last night and we are getting married today.' Her statement terribly smacked my heart, my heart beat had increased and my brain went numb. My feet were shaking and I was running all over my room, the call was still on and I was begging her not to take such an extreme step.

'Somu, it's over now, forget me forever. I never loved you, I just love Rakesh,' she disconnected the call and the number was switched off again.

The numbness in me had captivated all my senses and I lay on my bed under my blanket, I curled myself up there, burying my face in my hands. I cried and I cried, how long I don't know. I remained that way till Mom called me for breakfast. I wiped my tears quickly and rushed to the bathroom, Mom had been suspecting me for some time. In the bathroom, under the shower, I still could feel my tears with its warmth. Tears somehow failed to stop at all.

'Studying too late, *beta?* See your eyes are still red,' Dad said at the dining table.

Life with Pogo

'Happy birthday to you, happy birthday to you, dear Sam ...' sang the three idiots of my life, it was my twentieth birthday, a month later after Urvashi's marriage. I had become a recluse after our break up and so it was really a long time since we gathered in our bachelor's den.

'This goes for our *Devdas*, cheers!' everybody chimed in with Amey.

'It's over *yaar*, forget it,' I stirred.

'Don't you really miss her, anymore?' Pogo (Paramjeet) asked. The name was bestowed by Amey after the new cartoon channel and the reason; I guess I don't have to mention it. Thanks Amey, *it was really a pain, typing such a big name.*

'Nah!' I shook my head. 'I miss my N-70.'

'Ten thousand bucks is a lot of money.'

'Eleven thousand, nine hundred and fifty three, it was a music edition.'

Urvashi had once promised to be the first one to wish me ... and know! Why did she have to do this to me; I really loved her. I was constantly checking my cell for her call or a message. But ...

'Hello! Hello!' I answered to a call from an unknown number. But nobody was speaking. 'Oh God', I shrieked. There was no doubt in my mind who it was on the other side. It was the call I was anxiously waiting for ... I ran to the balcony.

'Hello! Hello!' I reiterated but still there was no response.

'Urvashi! I know it's you. Now, say something.'

'Hi! How did you guess, it's me,' she finally spoke.

'You know it better. Anyway does it matter? Tell me why you called?'

'As if you don't know?'

'See, there is no use playing such word games. Just shoot what you have to say, I got other people to attend to.'

'Really, Somu? You're so rude today.'

'I'm always like that only and my name is Samarth.'

'That was mean to say, just because I didn't go with you ...'

'What?' I interrupted. 'Urvashi! You're a bi*** ... forget it. You're not worth my abuses even. I hate you and I hate you. Just go to hell and don't dare to call me ever,' I shouted and disconnected the line.

'Who was it?' Amar asked me as I entered the hall again.

'Shalini,' I lied.

'Oh! really?' Amey asked me with a sarcastic tone.

'It was Urvashi but don't you worry, I've given her what she deserved.'

'What?'

'Forget it! Let's party,' I said and toasted up a bottle of beer 'Cheers!'

I always doubted beer being potent alcoholic material. For me it's a mixture of water, soda and women hormones. I mean after a bottle or two, you are just shaken off feet, talk rubbish and drive terribly but that day … I mean that night, the experience was a bit more powerful, and I could see "two" Amar dancing around. That's because my tank was filled till my neck and I still wanted to go on.

'Get over it, Sam! Don't cry because it's over but smile because it happened,' Amey said.

'Of course, I'm not regretting it even one bit, I'm celebrating,' I paused. 'But Amey, truly speaking, I miss her a lot. I don't know why she chose to do so.'

'Well see, at the end of the day she had a brain of a sixteen-year-old girl, it's easy to get influenced at that age. Girls are sentimental and dumb,' Amey said.

'I have a piece of advise for you,' Amar snorted 'Go to the bathroom and recall some of your incredible memories …'

'You're so cheap,' I bawled at him.

'What? As if you don't do it.'

∞

The party was over; it was late morning next day. Amar and Amey, had already vanquished and I looked around to realise why? Cleaning that whole mess that too on my birthday was not done at all, so I tried to go back to sleep again and an hour or so later when I opened my eyes, it was all gone. My trick worked!

'Good afternoon, Birthday boy!' Pogo greeted, I responded with a smile.

'Hey! You cleaned all the stuff,' I tried to give an astonished look.

'Of course!'

'Why didn't you wake me up?'

'It's your birthday today, how could I ask you to clean up the place. That would have been very mean of me. Anyway, not going to college today?' he asked.

'C'mon, it's my birthday?'

'Oh! don't give me that crap. In school, you used to wait all year for your birthday so that you could come in civil dress and distribute sweets; and now you don't even want to attend college for your birthday?'

'Yeah! It's only on a birthday, that you're not scolded or punished even if you don't do your homework. Wow Pogo! You still remember all that but then that was in school. And, when is your birthday?'

'Well, it's on 11th May, summer vacation time.'

∽

'Okay! Where is my gift anyway?'

'Let me think ... hey! You don't know how to ride a bike, right? (I nodded) my gift would be to teach you to ride one. Okay?'

'Sounds cool! When does the training start?'

We rode to the unused runway of the new airport. We were not alone though perhaps that place had been used for that very purpose only; one could only see bikes and cars all over with a 'L' sign. For Amey it was like crime and never missed teasing me on that, so I felt happy that I was not just alone, not knowing to *vroom* at the age of twenty.

'Leave the clutch slowly and at the same time race it too,' Pogo instructed sitting at the pillion and that also very close; his hands were over my shoulders and had almost reached my palms. His closeness had me a bit anxious recalling Amey's opinion about him and so the ride was not going that smooth.

'Change the gear, now,' he said and I looked down at my left to check on the gear.

'Look in the front, apply brakes,' he yelled. I quickly shifted to right to search for the brakes and found it. But it was too late, and bang ...

We dashed on the bricks, after slipping on the sand. Both of us were safe as we landed on the sand, just a few scratches on knees but the same could not be said for the bike which dragged a bit over the road to make some distance. Right indicator was gone with a big scratch on the headlight and the oil tank got in a bit; my training was over, I thought.

∽

'Sorry *yaar* for this,' I apologised, applying Dettol to my wound.

'Ouch!' he shrieked. 'It's okay! Life is full of ups and downs.'

Not again. I wondered why the hell each time, he ended up with such heavy lines. But if really I didn't want my dream to acquire a license not being shattered, so I had to bear and care.

'Anyway, tell me Pogo what happened to you. I mean ... why are you not staying with your parents,' I asked.

'Well, that's a bit personal,' he said.

'But you're my very close friend, I think I should share it with you,' he added.

'Yeah! That would be better,' I had to say.

'I always aspired to become a footballer and I'm sure I'll achieve my goal someday, for that I need to put on loads of effort and time too. But my Dad was not happy with it and that's when I failed. He was very angry and disappointed, he asked me to leave home if I still wanted to go ahead with the game and so I am here.'

'Hey! Your story is so much similar to mine but I'm fortunate enough that my parents gave me another chance.'

Perhaps, I thought Pogo was dumb enough to leave his parents for Football. Does he know in our country even the school peons earn more than footballers? His parents were right for sure but I had to take his side.

'That was bad; I mean they are your parents. How could they do this to you? They are so selfish.'

'Of course not, Sam. Rather, I guess I am selfish for choosing my passion over my family. I understand their side very well and love them very much. You see, my life revolves only around two things: one is selfishness and the other is empathy. Selfishness evokes the devil in me. It teaches me to live for myself. It takes me closer to hell whereas, empathy evokes the God in me. It teaches me to understand others. It takes me closer to heaven; apparently I'm stuck in between. Is this what they call earth?'

'Wow! That was cool but I didn't understand a bit of what he had said. How can you think like that?'

'Why? Just because I watch cartoons ...'

'No, nothing like that? I love them, too. Okay! I haven't seen your favourite movie, what was that ... Yeah, Brokeback Mountain. Do you have it?'

'Yup! But you won't like it.'

'C'mon, I said *na*, I love cartoon movies.'

'What?' he smiled. 'Okay, as you wish.' He had a very different and dodgy smile.

I had promised not to move till it ends ... I am talking about the movie, he was right; I didn't like the movie at all, perhaps it was a scary experience with Pogo around. No, no he didn't do anything but Amey's words regarding Pogo still haunted me.

'So, how was it?' he asked and I could just return a puzzled look. 'I have already told you; see, you people are not sensible enough to understand this.'

'What was so sensible in the film? A guy loving another guy, that's weird and loathly.'

'Sam, love is blind. And, do you know the movie won an Oscar.'

'I don't care about that and also don't want to argue any further on this but I think love is not that blind, not able to differentiate between a guy and a girl.'

∞

I tried my best to hate him even more. Except for the driving training, I ignored the rest of the time and we stayed separated from each other. But, he was always polite and kind. I thought it was kind of *Gandhigiri* from his side and finally I had to knuckle under to his good nature. Perhaps, I had started respecting him a lot. I didn't care whether he was loser, he watched cartoons or he was a gay. I never understood what really made Amey think like that. Pogo's thoughts were peculiar and his actions made him even weirder but then possibly, there were so many things I had to learn from Pogo. I appreciated that he was always honest and true. I had always ignored my instincts, exhorted my desires and in that way I had always been cheating, even to myself. Whatever I say to others, only I knew what music meant to me. It was greatest passion of my life. But my parents too thought the other way and I succumbed to that pressure, I gave in.

'Sam, I still remember the song you sang at the school function. Why don't you play guitar anymore.'

'Yeah! I do play it sometimes. After all, it's just a hobby.'

'Liar!' he smiled. 'Your story is also similar to mine'.

'So,' I reacted imitatively.

'The "Indian Idol" audition didn't mean the end to everything. Your passion deserves a lot more than that.'

'Forget it! I don't care about it anymore,' I urged.

'I saw it when it was aired ... I understand your pain but don't lose hope. You see, hope is God's mathematical equation. He tries to manipulate the equation to get what you want. Sometimes it works. Sometimes it doesn't. But we need to keep trying though.'

'No, in my case it's always zero. God hates me.'

'What? Sam, you're just impossible. It's really very simple to put the blame on God. You forgot the song, whose fault was it? You know God is present in everyone's heart. So, hating him means hating yourself.'

'Pogo, please ...' I pleaded or rather begged him to stop it.

'Okay! But then you've to come with me to the stadium today. I have an important match today.'

'No way ... Pogo, I don't like sports and than too football ... I don't understand a bit of it even,' I snubbed immediately.

'There is nothing to understand in that. After all it's not a bloody Maths class. You've to enjoy it,' he said but still I didn't budge.

'Come for me at least.'

What did he mean by that? He meant nothing to me.

'Okay! Then a ten kilometre ride after the match,' he offered. *That's better*, I nodded.

I've told you earlier that I don't understand soccer but is it all about rules? At least, it is not so in Mumbai. It was more like a rugby game, perhaps even more chaotic. Half of the players were clueless, not even sure for what they were on the field. I could completely understand why Indian Soccer is bankrupt. Considering all these facts, the crowd was rare, too minimal but I was really enjoying it. It was amusing and hilarious. But Pogo stood out brave, dauntless and different from the rest of the circus. He was like a star among them. He chased, dodged, grabbed and evaded perfectly. Out of the four goals his team scored, three came from his kick. No doubt, he had wasted a lot of time in mastering the game. Truly, it was thrilling to watch him play.

After the match ...

'So what do you think? How was it?' Pogo said.

'Cool! You play very well. So, let's go for the drive.'

'Yes! Of course,' he said and threw the keys to me.

'What?'

'You wanted to drive, *na*?'

'Yes but not here, duffer. Let's go to the airport.'

'Damn Sam! It's almost twenty kilometres from here.'

'And it's a highway here. Are you willing to go for a suicidal ride?'

'C'mon Sam, I trust you. You've been learning to ride since a week now.'

'But I don't have the confidence, *yaar*.'

'Don't tell me that and anyway I cannot drive, I sprained my ankle while playing and it's paining,' he said and limped a few steps.

'But you were alright, a second ago ...'

'Actually it started to pain just now,' he said.

'Really?' I said with dubious expression.

'Enough now *yaar*, nothing would happen. If I can trust you, why can't you trust yourself?'

It was in my childhood when an astrologer told my Mom that there are chances that I would meet with a major accident in my youth. And, that's why Mom had never allowed me to even linger around vehicles, forget driving. I only know how I learned, and later managed to ride a cycle. Perhaps, somewhere in my mind even I had a fear of that and so was frightened at Pogo's offer of driving all the way back. But that was the perfect moment for me to get over all my nightmares. So that was it, I was on the Mumbai–Pune highway.

It was noon, so the roads were quite empty. I was still apprehensive to leave the clutch and was just burning out the silencer.

'Asshole! Move on,' he shouted and get set go ... I was on road ...

'C'mon, Sam! Accelerate *yaar*, you are riding a Pulsar. Think of its dignity,' Pogo seemed too excited. I didn't understand why? But I was loving the joyride too. Might be I was averse, yet I did race high and the bike sped up, I was already nearing the hundred mark on the speedometer and almost overtook every vehicle on my way. The feeling of being brave and adventurous had triumphed over all my fears as I cut my way through the traffic confidently.

'Sam, stand up!'

'What?'

'Like this,' he said and was on his feet resting his hands on my shoulders. His feat freaked me off and I was losing my balance.

'What the hell are you doing?' I shouted.

'Shut up! Concentrate on the balance. Don't worry, nothing will happen.'

'Come down! I am scared.'

'Sam, you're a rat.'

We reached our building in a while. I parked the vehicle, I wanted to be happy after all I had driven all the way back home but Pogo's stunt had soaked all the blood out of my veins and I really didn't want to recall it. I remained quiet in the lift.

'Sam! Chill *yaar*, it's over now. See we're alive,' he laughed but I didn't respond. 'Please, talk to me now.'

'That was scary damn! Are you out of your mind? Don't you fear death?'

'Well,' he smiled. Something was in the pipeline for me. Oh my God!

'Life and death are two things that are surely bound to happen. I traverse death every moment. But I have never experienced the former. And I don't care for it at all.'

I didn't even try once to apply my brain to whatever Pogo said. I just did what I do most of the time, returned him a blank look. He understood and was laughing. I don't know whether he was laughing at me or at himself.

'To hell with him and his philosophy, I hate you Pogo', I thought to myself.

The Success

'What are you doing here in my bedroom?' I cried in anguish and quickly slipped under my quilt feeling very embarrassed as I was in my undies!

'What?' He looked puzzled at my actions.

'Get out of my room, now,' I ordered and he didn't dare to challenge. He left.

It was enough, the water had had reached over my head and I couldn't tolerate it anymore. He had reached my bedroom, how terrible was that? I wanted a complete explanation, I had to call Amey and first of all, I needed a new place, I was just going mad, wondering his motive.

'Sam! Are you fine?' he sneaked in his head from the door. I had clothed till then but was still in agony.

'I said stay away from me,' I shouted and threw my *chappal* at him.

'Hey! Chill *yaar*, what's wrong with you?'

'What were you doing in my room?'

'I was not here to steal something. I just came to give you this,' he passed me an envelope. I tore it open, it was my license.

'My friend in the RTO had called me yesterday and I collected it while returning from the stadium. I forgot to give it last night.'

'Really?'

'Then, what did you expect? I came here to see you lie naked?' He questioned. I kept quiet but my expression had conveyed the reply.

'What do you think of me Sam? Am I a gay? ... that's so mean of you Sam to think like that,' he stormed out of my room.

I checked the license and laughed, not thinking of Pogo's plight but at my horrible photo. Sometimes, I really act crazy. Amey is right about me, I am dumb. But then, hope is God's mathematical equation and you're aware of my chemistry with God.

'Hey! I am sorry,' I apologised.

'But that was really ridiculous. How could you even think of me like that?' He demanded an answer from me.

Even I don't know why Amey said that. He rarely justifies.

'Just because I like *Brokeback Mountain*?'

Maybe, I thought but I kept mum.

'Improve your level of thinking a bit dude,' he bawled at me. But thank God! That was it. No further lecture on life that day, perhaps he was in a different and jolly mood.

'What's the matter Pogo?' I asked but he didn't speak. He was busy packing his stuff for the stadium.

'Pogo, answer me.'

'Why should I tell you? You're not worth it,' he said and banged the door on my face.

'Go to hell', I muttered.

In the college, the lectures were as always boring and I was not able to concentrate at all. My mind was computing on a stream of thoughts which were no way related to Electronics. I was thinking about Pogo. Yes! About him. First of all, what was the matter? I had never seen him whistling around so happily. It had to be something big but he didn't tell me and I was curious. He never came to college. Was football that important for him? And most importantly, from where did he manage his expense, when his parents didn't care for him and were no longer funding for his studies.

'Meet me at the Ice & Spice, Seawoods after three,' read a SMS from Pogo.

⁕

'Cheers!' All of us tinkled our glasses.

'But what is the occasion Pogo?' Amar asked.

'It's a surprise,' he replied. It had to be a big surprise; otherwise Ice & Spice ... But who cared for the reason, it was the time to booze off!

'So guys ... the news is that I'm going to Kolkata. I have been selected in the National Football team.'

'What??' The three of us screamed out of shock, in unison. The word NATIONAL was too heavy to digest. It meant that you're a part of something which is better than the rest of the hundred million in the country.

'Wow! That's great *yaar*,' I complimented.

'I'm leaving today itself. I have to report at a training camp in Kolkata. I'm really thankful to my club here and also you guys, Amar and Amey,' he said. What? He did not mention my name; I narrowed my eyes and looked at him furiously.

'And special thanks to my roommate, you're lucky for me. Thank you Sam, thank you for everything,' he added.

'Flat-mate,' I corrected. Anyway Sam, I want you to start your music all over again,' Pogo said.

'Hey! Who are you to order me? Damn it *yaar*! Why can't you just mind your own business?' I hailed at him furiously.

'Chill *yaar*! It's okay!' But it wasn't okay, I know. He did feel bad. He deserved it, I consoled myself.

After the party, we accompanied Pogo to the airport. I was rude to him at the pub. Yes, I hate him but it was his big day ahead. I didn't want him to take any bad regards in the camp. I had to apologise, I had to bid him bye on a happy note, that's what etiquettes are, I guess.

'Hey! I am sorry Jeet,' that old name brought a beam on his face and came to hug me.

'Thank you, but call me Pogo,' he whispered in my ears. Amar and Amey raised eyebrows over that.

Two days past after he went to Kolkata, I lay silent on the couch. With nothing to do and staying alone, I was dying of boredom. There was nobody to fight with, nobody to shout on and nobody to hate. Was I really missing him? No not all or yes definitely, I was. I was getting used to my life with Pogo. What if Amar and Amey come to know about it? I had to get over the "missing Pogo" feeling soon.

I thought of checking out some porn stuff. But I had already watched them hundreds of times and now they didn't excite me at all! Then maybe, I should complete my journals. Bad idea! What will I do in the pre-exam leave then? Lastly, just one thing remained ... Music!

I dusted my music diary, quite a longtime! I browsed through the pages. The songs, the notes, the spot-ons and the remainders took me back to Danny's musical. I smiled recalling those golden days. I missed them dearly. Was I really out of touch? Yes, I was! I wanted to do something that made me happy. No reasons, no occasion, no motive, nothing ... I just wanted to get back to music because I loved music. It's my life and I should be deciding what is good and what is bad for me, I thought to myself.

I bought a guitar next day from the money I had saved for buying a bike. I bought an old acoustic though. I spend the whole day tuning and polishing it. I tried on it some composition of my few old works. It was a bit difficult but I had not yet lost my touch. The symphony of the a strings gave me strange solace. I played and I played, music always made me happy and why was I refraining myself from such a beautiful feeling, I wondered.

⁂

My sleep was disturbed by sounds from the hall and the kitchen. Thief! I rose immediately, I checked the time. It was 7.30 in the morning.

'Thief at this time,' I wondered, yet I sneaked through quietly, why take a chance! I took the broom in my hand for protection and headed towards the kitchen softly. And, I caught him.

'Pogo!'

'Hi there! Good morning.'

'How did you get in?'

'Don't forget, I too have keys for this house.'

'But you were to come on Saturday, right?'

'Yeah! For your kind information today is Saturday.'

'Oh! I am sorry ... I forgot to pick you up. It just slipped my mind. Tell me then, how did you manage to reach all the way here so early.'

'Oh! please, don't ask me about it ... what are you doing with this broom?'

'Oh! Nothing *yaar*. I was going to sweep the hall,' I lied.

'Really?' he smiled, I nodded. 'Do you think you can knock down a thief with just that broom? That's really very dumb of you to think like that!' We both laughed at my foolishness.

'Sam! So, you finally listened to my advise,' Pogo said seeing the guitar in the hall. I returned him a smile.'

'You know what that's really good because you still have two weeks with you,' Pogo said.

'Two weeks ... for what?'

'I want you to participate in the Bandwarz.'

'What? Have you gone out of your mind? Music is just a timepass for me.'

'Really?'

'Pogo! Please, I've suffered a lot for this in the past and I don't want it to happen all over again. I am not as brave as you. I would never go against my parent's wishes and they just want me to study, so that's it? And anyways, there is no chance of me being able to participate. It's "Bandwarz ... *band-war*" dear, and I am just one ... no band team. Okay!'

'Oh! don't worry about that, I've a friend who is a coordinator there. Your participation should not be a problem. And please, give it a last try *yaar*, just two weeks. Exams are four months away, you will still have enough time to prepare and study well.'

'But what would I do alone, I have no band, Pogo.'

'You know what you've to do,' he winked.

I didn't understand what Pogo meant to say but honestly I really didn't have any idea what to do. Thirteen days up and I was still blank. I'd thought of taking a piece of advise from Shalini, Amey or even Amar. But no! Something in me warned me not to tell them.

∞

I had started preparing for my performance; it was going to be different and eccentric this time. While the rest of the participants had an arsenal of instruments and orchestra, I was going to face some one thousand-odd audiences with just an acoustic guitar, that too a second-hand one. Whatever! I just wanted to enjoy the moment. It was dawning on me that this might be the last time I was ever going to get a chance to be on stage and I wanted to make it big. When the 'D' day arrived, I plucked on the strings and started singing the first few lines as a rap.

> *C'mon people juzz raise your arms,*
> *Like a toddler, never calm;*
> *Let go off the tension and then see,*
> *What to fly like a free bird be;*
> *C'mon converge and bellow,*
> *Pick up your phone and say "hello";*
> *Juzz don't think what others do,*
> *Or you'd feel u r in a loo ...*

I took a look at the audience ... they were not going groovy or crazy, unlike in other performances. Perhaps, there seemed to be a harmony of silence. What did it mean? Good or bad? But as my song progressed, I could see the audience enjoying humming the melody of words and tunes of my old string. That really got me going, I switched on my gears and what followed after that moment was complete madness of wild euphony from my strings.

And, at the end of it, the silence crept in again and then came a loud noise of applause. I started on with my guitar once again and this time I got a support from a few guys, who joined me with their instruments. It was drums, keyboard, percussions and my guitar competing with each other and their fusion made the atmosphere rock on ...

> *Jump up, jump down, twist like a fool,*
> *Feel like a monarch out to rule;*

Feel no shame be shameless now,
Come moan like an injured cow ...
Hear people how coarse I cry,
No throat like mine, so dry;
Howl and roar, jump and twist,
Tightly grab your partner's wrist;

Turn yourself off and on,
Roll out like a dog on the lawn;
Sense how loud can the music be,
So loud that the beats you see;
Come feel like an idiot clown,
Making faces to wipe your frown.
No wise human now here to see,
So be what you have'nt yet been;
Clap your hands like a child,
be harsh, be cruel, don be mild ...

As I ended my song, I could see almost everyone shaking to the tunes of my chords and they shouted ENCORE! I might not be the best but was not bad at all.

The result was out and I didn't win the competition. But I was not disappointed at all; I had given my best and was not bothered about the result. This was something I always yearned ... a stage performance and I had got an opportunity, so I was very happy. It was like a dream come true for me. Thank you, Pogo! Thank you for everything.

'Samarth Sinha, please come on stage,' I heard an announcement, it was my name. 'Was I hearing it right,' I wondered. The announcement was repeated and indeed, it was me. But why was my name being announced?

I went up to the stage; the anchor was talking about me, my song and my performance. The crowd cheered for me, the light moved with me and I approached the guests who were waiting for me. I was given a special prize, I was completely taken aback, it was something I least expected, somehow I managed to smile when I shook hands with the Chief Guest. I glanced at him; I thought I was familiar with the face behind that husky and bushy beard and the big hat. The bold light made it more difficult for me to recognise the person; moreover, I didn't care also who the Guest was. The euphoria of victory had triumphed over my curiosity and I ran down the stage, to be with my friends.

'Hey! Here is a note in it,' Amar said, as he tried to tear the gift-wrap.

'Amar, it's my gift and I was supposed to open it.'

'Sam, but see what is written in it.' "MEET ME BACK STAGE"

'So Sam, what are you going to do?' Amey asked.

I went to the changing room where the Chief Guest was waiting for me. He seemed to be too excited to see me.

'So Sam! How are you?' he asked. I was puzzled, how did he know my name!

'Somu!' he repeated my name again. 'Can't you recognise me?' He removed his hat.

'Oh! my God,' I literally shouted.

It was "DANNY" and I jumped with joy to give him a tight hug.

'What happened to you?' I asked Danny still astonished to see him.

'Well ... I have become a big man, now! Actually, I own the group "Nostalgia".'

'What? That new music company?' I was stunned. He nodded with a smile.

'Wow! Danny, that's great!' I was very happy for him.

'Sam! Music bonded us and see ... today music only has brought us together again. I'm so happy to see you again.'

'Same here, Danny. Today's night was once in a lifetime opportunity for me and I succeeded because of your blessings. I used your pluck turm ... my good luck charm,' I showed him the old little thing from my pocket.

'The big thing is still waiting for you, my child. I want you to do a music album for me.'

I didn't know how to react. My heart almost skipped a beat, I was completely taken aback. Danny hugged me. I pinched myself several times to realise that it was not a dream. And, I was actually standing in front of Danny, the owner of Nostalgia, with an offer of doing an album for him!!

'Oh! my God ... I was going to faint', I thought.

'Welcome to Nostalgia, dude.'

She is back

I knew Mom wouldn't understand it, so I kept this Album thing a top secret. I wanted to give her a surprise. Danny's offer to me was equally shocking for everyone who had heard about it like me. One has always been fascinated about the hi-fi lifestyle, the life of the stars and other elites who have gained popularity. Their fans, media attention, parties and functions, have always generated a sense of awe in the common man. Now I was going to be in the same league. Everything just seemed to be too good to be true for me ... it was now my chance to burn the stage. I was on cloud nine; I was living my dream. And, when dreams are big, facts don't count.

Danny had become a true professional. Our work was on the floors from day one. First, we selected the songs and set the tunes. And then, we were to record them and finally do the videos.

'Wow! I too would be in MTV soon', I rejoiced.

But I still didn't want to disappoint my parents and continued with my studies too. I would spend the morning at college and rush to the studio after that, spending hours there practising. The studio made my routine quite hectic and frantic. I would get completely exhausted at the end of it. At times, I did not even have the energy to exchange words with my friends. Yet I was not complaining. This was my dream; this is what I wanted to do all my life.

'*Lose control ... lose control ... I'm a rebel,*' my phone buzzed.

'Okay, I'll be there in 15 minutes,' I said and hung up.

'Danny, got to go. I have to meet someone.'

'Who ... girlfriend?' Danny asked.

'No, my boyfriend,' I beamed. It was Pogo. Danny looked at me with a dubious expression and I didn't wait to clear his doubts either. I was already late.

Pogo was waiting for me at the gate of Cinemax. Yes! We were going for a movie. No doubt, it had to be a cartoon film. It was a promise I made to Pogo. So, I was keeping my cool fervently even seeing penguins flying and hippos dancing. The movie was *Madagascar-2*.

'It seems, you guys are dating,' Amey joked. We bumped during the interval.

'No *yaar*, we are just friends,' Pogo reverted.

'Anyways, the job is done. I have made all the arrangements,' Amey said.

'About what?' I asked.

'Oh! I didn't mention it to you because you were busy with your music sessions. Actually, I bonded with my parents again and they are throwing a party to a few of our close relatives and friends in honour of me being selected for the national team'.

'And you finally won your battle. So, you're moving in with your parents again?'

'No, not now. This place is close to my college and the football ground. And, since the Indian team doesn't play that much, I guess

I will have enough time to complete my degree as well. What say?' He said with a pleasant and content smile on his face.

'Whoa ... that's cool, let's celebrate. Let's booze off,' I geared up.

'It's not always good to booze for slightest reasons. It will affect your health. Booze to celebrate and don't celebrate to booze.' There was a bit of cynicism in his words.

'C'mon, guys.'

'Sam! Are you happy that Pogo has bonded with his parents or are you happy that he is staying back with you?' said Amey.

Sometimes, Amey is so irritating.

'Shut up! You asshole.'

'Don't fight *yaar*. Anyway, Sam! I have a big surprise for you. Dress properly for the party, okay?'

༄

My days became even more busy and frenzied as the deadlines for the release came nearer. The team at Nostalgia were all working hard for the album; at times they even behaved like zombies running around. And, Danny had completely gone mad. My life was completely screwed and everything seemed to be going out of my mind ... and the worst part was I forgot about Pogo's party!

There were fifteen missed calls, nine messages and also my phone was tired of buzzing the remainder, I saw as I checked my mobile in the locker. Oh my God! Pogo would kill me for this. I rushed to the parking, took my bike and sped up to reach Pogo's house. I remembered Pogo's words to dress up nicely but how would my dressing matter, I wondered. *After all, Pogo doesn't even have a sister to impress.* Forget it! What you are wearing is just fine, I comforted myself. So, there I was, wearing a white shirt which had turned pale yellow over the week and a worn out and tattered jeans. My hair was messy, face dry and I was wearing my floaters instead of shoes. My antagonism with the shower is already known to all and worse today, I didn't even get a chance to spray some deodorant ... God help the party animals, I prayed.

'You're so late, dear,' Amar said.

'You should have taken a bath at least,' Amey sniffed.

'I guess so but I didn't get any time. I came directly from the studio. I'll leave once I meet Pogo, okay!' I said.

'Hello Sam!' Pogo came in.

'Hi. Nice party dude.'

'But why have you come like this ... your clothes are so dirty. I told you to dress decently *na?*'

'I was busy yaar ... anyways, I'm not staying here much ... just dropped in to wish you. So, now tell me fast what was the big surprise that you were harping about the other day.'

'No way, forget about it now,' Pogo denied it straightaway. Just then ...

'Jeet! Jeet!' a sweet voice came from behind.

I turned back to look who it was and ... *oh my God! Am I seeing right?* I rubbed my eyes, I couldn't believe. *Is it the same girl, I'm thinking? Or, is it someone else? Is it Shamita?*

'Shamita?' I asked the gorgeous lady standing in front of me. I checked her out she was just the same, except that she was not wearing anything pink! She was wearing a knee-length black dress and trust me; there was no one else in the party matching even a percent to her enigmatic beauty.

'Excuse me! Do I know you?' she said. *How could she forget me?* Horrible ... how mean of her.

'Shamita ... I am Samarth Sinha. I was with you in school. I gave you a purple water bottle on your birthday, remember?' I was so excited to see my first love.

'Excuse me!' She gave me a dirty look. I understand, that was really hapless, first you give such a cheap gift and then you try to remind her about it ten years later, that too in front of a hundred people! Phew, way to go man, I chuckled.

'Yes ... yes, I remember now. You're the *Mamma's Boy*.' The word was not that offensive but it did turn a few heads towards me. Amey and Amar were already smirking down lowly. I gave a furious look to Pogo; after all, he only gave me the name. Oh! I hate you Pogo.

⁂

'That wasn't my fault. I told you to dress up properly,' Pogo said defensively. From the past few days, everything between us ended up on the same argument.

'She called me Mamma's Boy. How mean was that?'

'Then go and fight with her. Why are you eating my brain?'

'It's your entire fault, accept it. You did it purposely.'

'What do you mean by that? Perhaps, I wanted both of you to come along but you screwed up the moment completely. Couldn't you take a bath at least?'

'Fuck off!'

A minute of silence between us and then it started again.

'C'mon, forget her now. She already has a boyfriend.' His tone being quite gentle.

'Then, why did you want both of us to meet?'

'Well, I can't say. I thought you would be happy to see her again. I know that you loved her once.'

'Really? Thanks for your concern. But I think she is not my type of gal at all now.'

'What? Do you even have a type. Sam! Just think once before you say something,' he said with a very mischievous smile. That's it! It was enough now. I jumped on him and dunk his head in the pillow. I just didn't want him to breathe anymore. He tried to rise but I had parked my large butt on his back, he struggled and grunted hard but I didn't let him go.

Enter Amey ...

'Oh oh ... it seems we are at the wrong time ... seems you are enjoying yourselves, guys!' Amey made a bolt from the blue sort of entry.

༄

My album was released in June that year. It was not just my efforts; I had to give the credit to everyone from my team. Thanks to my University Papers, I couldn't attend the launch party and also the press conference. But actually, I was happy missing them. I had learned to balance my both lives, I could prioritise things around well, now no more disasters because I knew what was important for me at what time. The result was quite good. My parents were happy and they had started understanding me. Though the result was not out but I was confident that I had reached final year and just the last hurdle remained to overcome, then I would be free forever. A year more of struggle and then no more college, no more ATKTs, no more submissions, no more expectations, nothing; it would just be Nostalgia and nothing else. My life was on a stable and successful march.

'Sam! I think you must change your Orkut initials now,' Amey suggested.

'Yeah! I too think so,' I said as I added the eighth friend request of the day. It was early to say whether my album was a hit but yes, my music was getting popular. It's hardly been a week after the release, and already there was a community dedicated to me, that too with over three thousand members! Phew ... Not bad at all! And, it was just not Orkut; I got fans from all around buzzing me. Moving in public had become difficult, I always got recognised. And, I completely loved all the young girls' attention/love for me. I always let them hug me, jump over me and kiss me ... I cherished each moment.

'Hello!' I picked an unknown call. No, it wasn't Urvashi.

'Can you guess?' *Please! I'm just fed up of this nonsense.*

'See, I got a lot of work to do. Say your name or hung up!'

'Attitude, huh!'

'Whatever you say, I don't care. I am keeping down the phone, bye.'

'Okay! Okay! Hang on. It's me, Shamita.'

'What? Shamita!' I was stunned, not possible at all. 'See, enough of your pranks. I don't like it even one bit.' I was sure, it had to be a prank played by one of my friends. I looked at Amey but he looked calm and normal. He's a good actor, though.

'Hey! You gave me that water bottle, remember,' she said. Not a big deal, Amey knows it all.

'Sorry, I don't remember.'

'That's very rude. How could you forget the New Girl? And, we had played chess at your friend's place, what's her name? I don't remember ...' she hit a bingo! So Madam remembers everything.

'Shalini! Is it really you, Shamita?'

'Yes *baba*, it's me Shamita. I watched your music video; I must say somebody was looking very handsome.'

'Oh! Thank you very much but how did you get my number.'

'Jeet gave me.'

'Yeah! Are you in Orkut?'

'Of course! I am.'

'I'll definitely add you.' I paused. 'So ...'

'You want to know why I called,' she said.

Certainly! I just wanted her to say it; I knew her motive.

'Can we meet?'

C'mon, princess, how can I say no to you? But I had become smart enough not to be carried away. Now, it was my chance to enjoy all the attention and popularity.

'Actually, I'm a bit busy these days. Let me see if I can take out some time for you ... ,' I tried to feign.

'It's okay! We'll catch up some other time then.'

'C'mon *yaar*, you are my old friend. I cannot disappoint you.'

'No, not all. I completely understand. Don't bother much about it.' She was really giving me a hard time to decide something fast ... else I was going to lose her again forever.

'Please *yaar*, we will meet this Saturday,' I urged.

'Okay! If you insist,' she had won it again. I felt like such a big loser.

She was deceivably smart than what I had thought her to be and I was still not sure about her intentions, but I was happy, she was my first love after all. I had waited for this opportunity for a long time and didn't want to get over the feeling. I quickly browsed through Orkut to check her profile. But before that, I got three more friend requests to think on. I instantly rejected the two guys and clicked on the third one, not because she was a lady but she seemed to be someone I knew. She was the owner of my fan club. *Maggie* was her name, strange! Her profile was a perfect mismatch to what she actually was. Her album had over 150 photos but none of her, not even of anyone to whom I could relate her with. There were monkeys, crows, shadows of human figures, landscapes, old castles, trees, creepers and all of them dark and spooky. I still added her all the same, don't know why!.

'Thank you.' I received a scrap. She was online but I didn't reply.

'I'm a big fan of yours,' she scrapped again. This time I replied with a thank you and she reverted a chat request. Reluctantly though, I accepted it, I had to be humble to fans.

Maggie: Hi ☺

Me: Hello

Maggie: I m ur big fan

Me: Yes I knw ☺ Thanx 4 d com

Maggie: Thanx 4 addin

Me: Ur profile is so dark and conservative. It seems u r a very—ve person

Maggie: M I?

Me: Ya but I knw u r beautiful

Maggie: Really Y u think so

Me: Dunno I just think so

Maggie: U r a very handsome guy 2
Frankly speaking I've a huge crush on you

Me: Thank you Madam
I'm flattered ☺

Maggie: do u hv a gf

Me: nopes ☹

Maggie: liar
k GTG ciao bye ☹

ॐ

Saturday arrived; we were to meet for dinner in the suburbs. It was not just dinner, I was to date her but Shamita was so sophisticated to use the word. Anyway, it hardly mattered. I had learned a lot from my past relationship and I didn't want to mess up this one, too. I had to make an impression on her from the day one itself and I prepared myself for it perfectly. I tried to analyse everything. High brands but formals were my choice to dress up and a small dial 'Fastrack' wrist watch which I bought for her as a gift; I had chosen a watch with a pink strap! Last time I had made a mistake, and this time I didn't want to.

'Cool,' her reaction was a bit cold than what I had expected.

'You liked the gift, *na?*' I inquired.

'Of course, the watch is great but the colour,' she said point blank.

'But I was under the impression that you love pink.'

'I used to but not any longer. I prefer black these days.'

'In school, you would never move around without anything that wouldn't be pink in colour.'

'Tadaaa,' she struck a pose. 'I'm nineteen now, tastes change.'

What did she think? I am a fool or what? She is ten days elder to me and I have already celebrated my twenty-first birthday and she is still nineteen. Only girls can come up with such nonsense, I guess.

'Tell me Sam! Have you ever gone out with somebody before?'

'Of course, I and Pogo, I mean Jeet, we party quite regularly,' I replied knowing very well what she meant.

'No, I mean do you like someone.'

'Yeah! I like all my friends. You see, other than Pogo there is Amar and Amey, they are all so adorable. You must meet them.'

'*Na baba,* I meant any woman in your life,' she sounded irritated by then.

'My Mom. I love her so much, that's why they call me ...'

'Sam! You're so impossible,' she cut in. 'Just tell me what you think about me.'

'What? I thought you've a boyfriend.'

'Are you talking about Yogesh? (Though I didn't know him, I nodded) C'mon we are just friends.'

'I guess that's a good news for me then.'
'Oh! You're such a flirt,' she said with a mischief in her eyes.
'And, you're such a slut,' I muttered lowly under the breath.

I *love you*

'Hello, Sam!'

'Pogo! Where are you?'

'I am in Delhi. Coming to Mumbai in another two hours,' Pogo said.

'Sir, please, switch off your phone,' a sexy voice was politely interrupting him.

'Pogo! Are you in the plane?'

'Yup,' he grunted.

'So, keep the phone.'

'It's okay *yaar!*'

'No. It's not okay, I'm busy. Actually, I'm with Shamita. We will talk later.'

'What are you doing with her? See, she is not a good girl.'

'Pogo! Please, I'll decide about that. Bye now.'

'Listen ... listen ...'

I cut the call. He called me again. What was so important, I wondered. I didn't want to know and I didn't want to think about it either. Shamita was looming around in that black sari which had white chicken embroidery work all over. What really makes women in sari, so aphrodisiacal? You see no hooks, no buttons, no knots, sari makes it all so easy. I just needed to pull her *aanchal* aside and … touch them … but Pogo …! I cursed him. I threw the damn phone on the floor and got into my private moment with her. I hugged her, eased my hands behind her back and pulled the knot of her blouse. Rest …

That was actually my third; with her it was the third time. But still, she would prefer to say we were just moving around together and not dating. And, this happened in the first week of our friendship only. But she kept saying no love *baba*, we are just friends. And later it was, we were just seeing each other, no commitment whatsoever. Yet, I was successful to seduce her to bed or she did it to me. Whatever, it was just more than awesome making love with her …

I smiled as I looked at her, Shamita was deep asleep. I guess it's more tiring for girls. And, who says male dominate it all? With her, I was a baby gazelle and she was the hungry lioness. I was a hapless kill and she, the malicious predator who had gone wild. A luscious voice of experience suited her well than a slut. Just one album of mine was out, that also a month ago and already the hottest chick, I'd ever encountered was lying naked besides me. Was it really that simple? I know how much I have struggled to reach that position of success, so I deserved everything nice. The pain, isolation, emotions, friendship and care had all turned my world upside down and I'd reached at the pinnacle where I always desired to be. But that was not the end, it was just the beginning and I had to move ahead even more sternly. Then, what was stopping me?

I checked my watch, it was 5.30 p.m. I was late again; I had a concert to attend. I glanced at her for a moment before leaving and I guess I got the answer to my last question.

∞

Let me be banned and fatal,
The easy short route,
If on those stroll my opposite mates,
I would dare not tread it, be I dead.

Let whatever in this world,
Come to me and compel,
I would seldom make it meagre my tell;
But it would lay tacit,
My intentions meanwhile,
That my sense and consciousness,
Has yet not been out to while;

But it'd be legal and safe,
The lone long course,
On which I stumble upon thorns
And be laughed aloud like a fool;
And for that which it may neither
Be embarked or strolled,
Nor be it in a plight to tread.

And on with every lumber,
My feet then, crooked,
Would curse and curse me all the way ...

212 Mom says no Girlfriend

But i'd never be so glad,
I saved myself from vice,
I diverted my mind,
I healed my wound for sure ...

And with each step I dawdle,
I keep to me my vow,
I be raised in my veiw,
I let me be in peace.

I scale the safe path,
Let it take my life to scale,
But would've rather chosen death,
Than a meagre walk,
On those pieces of stone,
Wherein I be cheated
Yet for a tragic/an encore ...

It was the most popular song of my album.

'That was awesome,' the organiser congratulated.

'Thank you very much. It was my pleasure singing here,' I said and marched to my dressing room.

'Hey Samarth! Wait!' Somebody called from behind. I turned, another fan!

'Hello! What's your name?' I smiled at him.

'Hey! I am Subho. Don't you recognise me?' He seemed surprised but I couldn't recall his face. I shook my head.

'C'mon, I'm Subho, the author of *Bowled N The Beautiful*.'

'What's that?'

'It's my first novel.'

'So ...'

'So … you still don't know me, that's so dumb. I mean, we all are young artists and probably should know and respect each other.'

'Well I am not into reading that much. Maybe, that's why I …'

'It's okay,' he cut in. 'Can you give me an autograph. My niece is a big fan of yours,' I could sense the disappointment in his voice.

'Sure,' I took his notepad and scribbled my name.

'Thanks,' he turned to go.

'Subho!' I called. 'Autograph please,' I spread my palm; I know how it feels to give an autograph.

∽

Pogo had returned, I knew but the lights were still off. I switched on the lights; he was lying on the floor bare chest. I called him. He looked at me. His face was pale and his eyes were swollen and blood red in colour. He was definitely crying. I scanned the rest of the area—blade, all-out mosquito repellant, clothes. What was he up to?

'Pogo is everything okay? I asked. He didn't reply. I went near him and put my hand on his shoulders. 'What happened *yaar*?'

He hugged me and started sobbing.

'What's wrong?' I comforted him.

'Where were you? Your phone was switched off and I was worried.'

'I told you. I was with Shamita. What was there to worry?'

'You slept with her?' he questioned, there was a different kind of seriousness and concern in his eyes.

'Why are you so much bothered about it?' I said sternly.

He lowered his face and didn't reply to that.

'What's the matter Pogo, please tell me? What's all these stuff?'

He was silent again.

'I'm worried for the results,' he said.

※

The results were out and it was official that I was at last promoted to the final year. Pogo too, managed to scrape through. Whatever, the battle was almost won. It was time for celebration; particularly it was the time to booze!

Finally Amar was hooked too. Don't know from where but yes! He had managed one partner and she was really pretty. I and Shamita were still *seeing each other*. But Pogo was still single. I thought of bringing Shalini and Pogo together but she refused to get into any relation for the time being. Instead, she introduced her friend Tina, who seemed to have a big crush on Pogo.

'Hi! Paramjeet,' said Tina enthusiastically.

'Hello!' Pogo replied rather coldly.

I didn't know whether the girls were aware of the fact that alcohol contained a high amount of fat which was enough to let them gain those extra pounds and screw their curvy figures. But I guess, the case was not so as they were sipping down cocktails one after another. Learn from Shalini, she never drinks! Of course, I was very concerned, the bill was on me!

'Let's dance,' I tried my best to divert them from the drinks. Everybody was game to dance except for Shalini who refused to dance either. Love really hurts ... I guess.

On the dance floor, everyone was going groovy and dandy over the hip-hop music. The alcohol had made its impact. Tina was really going wild; I think she lad lost it completely ... she tore open Pogo's shirt and was literally all over him. Pogo seemed very uncomfortable by her actions and tried his best to move away from her.

'I am feeling tired. I want to sit for some time,' Pogo excused himself and went to sit on a sofa placed in a far corner. He was lost in some thoughts and wanted some privacy. But Tina thought the other way. She downed a few pegs of cocktail and comforted herself on his lap and ... all of a sudden started kissing him. I couldn't take my eyes off them and so were the other couples at the bar glaring at a freeshow! How lucky Pogo was? I was jealous of him. But Pogo was not at all excited and remained still throughout as if it were some sort of a punishment. And, I thought such punishment would make even a dead man dance but Pogo ... something bad was to follow, I reckoned.

'Just stay away,' Pogo pushed Tina down, on the floor. She was lying on the floor and there was a dead silence at the night club and everybody was staring at them. Embarrassment at its best, I wondered!

'What do you think of yourself?' she burst in rage. 'You're such a loser in life. I don't know why I fell for a moron like you. People are right about you, you indeed are ... a gay. Girls save your guys from him,' he hurled at him.

Shalini came forward to stop her but she was going on and on. Pogo didn't say a word. He just looked down trying to avoid an eye contact with everyone. Finally, with the help of the bouncers Shalini was able to take Tina outside. We too were thrown out of the pub following the incident. I wanted to stay with Pogo, I knew he was hurt but Shamita was with me. Leaving your girl on her own to return home, is never expected from good boyfriends like us, even if your friend has got a bullet right on his chest. So, we all went with our respective partners while Pogo left alone for home. I know it was really very mean of me to leave him alone but I couldn't help.

When I returned, Pogo had already gone to bed. I wanted to talk to him and know if he was okay, but ... was he crying? I was not sure, he had covered his face with the blanket and I thought it was better not to disturb him at that point. I switched off the lights of his room and went to my room.

'Why was Pogo cynical towards all these advances; what's really wrong with him; why couldn't he be like us, have fun and enjoy', all these questions kept hovering over my head and denied me any sleep. I was really very upset for Pogo.

I thought of browsing through the net a bit to kill some time. I logged in Orkut and a green dot appeared on my profile. I tried to change the status but it was too late.

Maggie: Hi ☺

Me: Hello

Maggie: Wassup yar?

Me: F9

Maggie: hw was ur day 2day?

Me: quite ok

Maggie: Y r u so dul 2day? Is evrythin ok Dere?

(Wow! That was really clever. But how did she know about it? Oh my God! Another Amey.)

Me: wat do u do? Don tel me u studin Psychology!

Maggie: no way, I m doin a course in fashion designing.

Over the months our friendship had grown and we had started sharing our problems with each other, too. And so, I told her everything that happened that night. Though I didn't tell her anything about Shamita ... *for obvious reasons.*

∽

Since that night, Pogo had gone into a shell. He hardly spoke to anybody and avoided all sort of gatherings. His silence over Tina's words had raised many eyebrows and he became the hot topic in the gossip chart. Whispers followed him all over, sometimes people would mock directly on his face but he was always mum. Even I didn't understand why was he not fighting back? He was the one who taught me to be brave and to learn to stand up for yourself. What was really bothering him? I hoped for things to be normal again. People's memory is so weak but Pogo's silence was not letting them forget it.

'Hi! Pogo,' I greeted as he returned from the gym.

'Hello,' he replied bleakly.

'Are you angry with me, Pogo?'

'No *yaar*, I'm angry with myself.'

'See Pogo, I fail to understand you; I don't know what is the matter with you; whatever it may be I leave it you; stand up for yourself; I know you can handle it.'

'Thanks for caring so much.'

'Please, now don't embarrass me. Anyway, I got two tickets for a movie. Anybody interested?'

'No, I am tired. Take your Girl.'

'Yeah! I'm thinking so but I guess she won't like the movie. After all, it's Batman Dark Knight.'

He could not say no to it, he was waiting for it longtime. I had stopped watching such sort of films but that was something Pogo loved and I just wanted to cheer him up a bit. Perhaps, it is sometimes very relaxing to revisit one's childhood days and be a kid all over again.

'So, what do you have to say, Pogo? Batman is simply the best.'

'He can't fly like my Spiderman.'

'Oh! you're so pathetic. Does your Spiderman have a car like this?'

My phone was vibrating since long, but I ignored it. I checked it, Shamita calling. I didn't pick, the movie was too engrossing to divert and attend the call.

My phone buzzed once again. It was a message now from Shamita.

'It's my Birthday today. How could you forget?'

Birthday? I checked my watch it was 16 November but I didn't ponder on that. The movie had reached its climax and it had become too engaging to miss. I switched off my phone. The movie ended. I wished it was not the end of the series. Anyway, the movie was a perfect five according to my ratings.

'Sam! Where are you?' she shouted at me as I called her after the movie.

'Sorry, sweetie! I was busy.'

'Come to Raigad Resort right now!' she ordered.

That was some 30 km away from Vashi. At times, girls are so demanding, they don't mind you breaking traffic laws and risking your life for the sake of their happiness. And still, they would claim that they care for us.

'It's been two hours since I've been waiting for you here,' Shamita was fuming. The number of coffee cups on her table proved she was not lying. She had reserved a small section just for the two of us. I hoped the bill wasn't on me!

'I am sorry darling.'

'I'm not talking to you. You forgot my birthday.'

'How can you expect me to remember your birthday when you look that pretty always? I don't think you can get old ever; instead, you are becoming prettier and prettier each day,' I caressed her and gave her a bear hug. I knew I was forgiven. Girls love to hear praises about them no matter what.

'But I thought your birthday is in July?'

'That is my original birthday. Today is my passport date birthday,' she said. And now, what's that? She has two birthdays in a year and she was still not ageing. It's really ridiculous but I was still entertaining her.

'Where were you anyways?'

'I was in the studio,' I lied.

'It's Sunday.'

'Well sweetie, I went to watch Batman with Pogo.'

'What? You, what? You went to watch that gay movie.'

'What do you mean?' From the past few days, I was just fed up of hearing that word all the time.

'I mean Batman is gay. See, every super hero has a girlfriend but he doesn't. He just moves around among men.'

She really possesses a brain of a size of a nut. I was damn frustrated at her statement. Why the hell did I have to tolerate her nonsense so much?

'Sweetie, leave it. Let's cut the cake,' I said, as the waiter brought in the cake she had ordered.

'It's not over yet, Sam,' she shouted at me. The waiter was still in an audible range.

'Please honey, I beg you to stop.'

'I care for you a lot and I really fear it.'

'What?'

'I mean your relationship with Paramjeet. Didn't you hear what Tina said that night?'

'She was drunk and I guess she is mad too.'

'But that's the truth. He is a gay and I want you to be away from that asshole.'

'Mind your language! You don't know what he means to me. I am what I am today because of him.'

'Oh! So, you care so much for that bas****. You're fighting with me for him?

It's been always amusing for me to watch women abuse like that but that day it hurt me badly. I'm very bad when I'm angry. The same astrologer had said that I have a hidden violent stride and unfortunately for Shamita, she seemed to have exactly hit on that. I was not thinking much, I just wanted to shut her loud mouth and the first thing that came to my notice was the cake on the table. I picked it up on my palm and dunked it right on her face.

She was shell shocked. Her mouth was wide open ... but no sound ... or reaction either, she stood dead, she did not even shriek. I could see tears from her eyes making its way down through the cream all over. But neither was I regretting nor was I feeling any guilt. None of us said anything after that mishap. I just ran away from that place. I don't know what happened to her after that; we never met since then.

I was more furious than being sad. But why? Why was I caring for Pogo so much? I didn't know. It was really so mean of me to behave like that with Shamita. I was ashamed of myself. I stopped my car at the wine shop, bought a bottle of vodka and some soda and returned to the flat.

'Hey! How was your date?' Pogo asked. I didn't reply to him and headed straight for my room. He too came in.

'What's the matter, buddy?' I didn't want to share what happened. I produced a fake smile, so that he wouldn't notice my discomfort.

'Pogo, it's not always we booze to celebrate, sometimes you have other reasons to drink. And, maybe at times, you drink just to forget something that you don't wish to remember.'

'Is everything okay with you? Did you fight with Shamita?'

'Don't ask me anything. Let's drink! Cheers!'

A bottle is more than enough for two to land among the stars. I was drowsing recklessly but still wanted to down more pegs.

'Sam! We should stop I think,' Pogo said in a shaky voice.

'Don't stop me today; I want to finish the bottle; do you have anything that will keep me awake?'

'Yes! A new DVD of Lacie Heart that will take you straight to heaven,' Pogo smiled.

Lacie Heart has been our all time favourite porn star; we hardly missed any of her videos.

'Pass me one more drink.'

Both of us had gone full tipsy and our body refused to stuff in further but still *yeh dil maange more*. I don't remember how it started. We were completely drunk and the porn had made our mind erotic. I looked at Pogo; he was peering at me with a smile. I smiled back too. He drew his hands towards me and slipped through my face. The feel of his hands aroused me. He then slowly approached me and kissed me, on my lips. *It's just a bad dream*, I said to myself ...

I was woken early in the morning by a call from Mom. I hadn't gone home that weekend. But before I could pick the call, I realised Pogo's arms were around me. I quickly threw them apart, it was not a dream. I was outraged to know about it. I was aghast ... how could I ... O God ... I repented. What had I done? But what is this ... we still had our clothes on us ... so everything was not as bad as I had presumed, I tried to pacify myself; we had not gone extreme for sure. Yet, as far as I remember, we had kissed and that was too an offensive act if it is between the same sex. My head was going tizzy, recalling my last night stint, a sense of hangdog engulfed me. But what hurt me more was that everyone was right about Pogo. He indeed was GAY.

'Sam! Sam!' he muttered, Pogo was coming to senses and didn't take much time to comprehend the matter. He quickly rose on his feet.

'See, I can explain,' he said.
'Just shut up. What is there to explain now?'
'Sam! I wanted to say that I love you.'
'What the F ... you bastard!!', I slapped him really hard right across his face with all my strength.

The Empathy and the Selfishness

'Cut it. What's happening Sam? Concentrate, I cannot give a whole damn day to record just one song,' Danny shouted.

That was the ninth take. God Damn! I was forgetting my lines each time, what was wrong with me? I had hit Pogo very hard, he was bleeding. Oh! What was I thinking? I just could not get out of it. It's been four days since that night; we hadn't met or talked with each other but not for a fraction of second was he out of my mind. I was missing him desperately. Again, I was caught in a situation where I could not talk or discuss with anybody. Our friendship was dead. To hell with him!

But I could not concentrate at all, howmuchever I tried not to think of that night; I couldn't. I continued with my mistakes and finally, Danny called it a quits for the day. I sat at the Vashi station, watching people getting in and off the train, rushing through the subways and moving around. Life is so busy for them, it's just not about fun and it meant so much to them, I wondered. I've always loved the aura of the place, I and Pogo used to often come over here for some relaxation. *Not again!* Whatever, I was determined to end the feeling once for all and for that *I called him!*

He was busy on another call, I tried a couple of times more and finally gave up. I was unable to understand myself; I wanted to forget him and here I was calling him, how silly was that! Just then my phone buzzed, Pogo was calling. *Don't pick up!* Was my first thought and I didn't pick. He called again and I ignored. But he kept calling. Suddenly, everything seemed to fall in place, Pogo was crying the other night because he was jealous of me being with Shamita. His feelings were not something instantaneous, it had been developing for some time and I never understood. Somewhere, I feared that he might take the extreme step again and I wanted to save him.

'Why weren't you picking my call?' he asked frantically.

'Who the hell are you to ask me that?' I hailed back.

'Sam! Let's meet. I want to sort out things between us.'

'What are you going to sort out now? Damn! Do you have an idea even what you have done?'

'Please *yaar*, meet me once. Come to the flat in the evening.'

'No way, how could you think that I will agree to it. I can't trust you anymore. You are a ...' I stopped myself from saying it.

'You can say whatever you want to, I don't mind at all. But please, come home, I will wait ... he continued but I hung up.

I knew thinking about the same crap again and again wouldn't help the situation. I lost all my appetite and knew that I had to take care of the situation; I couldn't let it go out of hands like this. I couldn't run away from it, I had to face it. There was nothing to fear, it was not my mistake and I wouldn't let these things smother me further, I decided. I'm brave enough; I would meet him and put an end to our friendship finally.

'I knew you would come,' he said.

'Just shoot fast, I've to go early.'
'Where?'
'My home.'
'So, you're leaving this place. (I nodded) And, what are you going to say at home? C'mon, Sam! Grow up; you know it's good here. College is near; your studio is too close. It's comfortable from here.'
'But I have to pay a big prize for that.'
'What do you mean?'
'You know what I mean.'
'You're misunderstanding the whole thing. It was just an accident.'
'Really?' I was stunned at his words. 'Then, what is all this? I mean you remember what you had said, rather confessed the other day?'
'Well,' he swallowed some saliva in. 'That's true actually. I really love you.'
'What? Are you still drunk?'
'No. I am not. Let me tell you what love for me is! Love is knowing you're never yourself, sharing stories till you tire, togetherness forever, having someone to share your life, hanging one to every word you say, waiting for you to return and it's the closeness that melts all fears away, something I know I've found in you. And, that's why I love you.'
'See, I know you're very good in all these things. It really doesn't impress me anymore okay ... what am I saying? I mean we both are guys, *yaar*, it's something unnatural.'
'What is unnatural? Love? Love has to be true and never fade away but always stay forever and ever. And now, peep into your life, I mean the girls you thought you were in love with, is anyone with you now. But love never ends.'

'So what? There are always hiccups in life. And, I don't think the other way, I am not ... I don't feel anything for you.'

'Really? Then why did you fight with Shamita for me?'

'Because she was wrong ... I thought at that time. Perhaps, everyone was right about you but it was only me who thought that you were not like that and I really hated them for what they used to say about you.'

'See, now you understand that you are the only one who cares or feels for me; this is exactly what I have been trying to make you understand.'

'Enough with your definitions of love!' I was frustrated now. 'See, Pogo! Can't we just remain friends like we were before? I mean why does this love thing have to come between us?'

'Of course, we are gonna be friends forever. I know what you are thinking about? You're confused about sex and love. Sam! Please, I told you that the kiss was an accident and my love is not bound to sex. It's more platonic for me. For me, love and sex are both different things. I love you but that does not mean that I want to have sex with you? I don't need anyone else in my life because I find all the qualities that I was looking in my soulmate in you, so what if you're a guy. I told you love is blind.' His statements and justification still were not able to budge me.

'Okay! Whatever you wish, we remain just friends. Just forget everything, let's make the things around us all the same as it was before.'

'Pogo! Things can never be the same as before because I now know what you feel for me.'

'Sam! Please, *yaar*, don't talk like that. Don't leave me alone,' he begged. Pogo cried. I was numb. I couldn't just see him cry.

I stayed back, the reason was never sure. The college is near and the studio is close by, I said to myself. Things between us never remained the same as before, everything had changed. We were even more close to each other though we slept in different bedrooms. Our relationship was limited to just a walk, hand-in-hand, sharing a comfortable silence, spending each moment as if it were the most precious.

All the togetherness lasted for just one year till we graduated. There was no more excuse to continue to stay in our bachelor's den yet, we decided to move on with the same feelings for each other. I trusted him, cared for him, missed him and liked him more than just a friend. But I knew such relationships had no future, we were at the pinnacles of our respective careers, and just a whiff of it need to leak outside and that would have signalled an end to all our career ambitions and dreams. Moreover, we also had our own families to look on to. Pogo was right, our life revolved around two things—selfishness and empathy. We chose empathy and separated our ways but decided to catch up during weekends, go for movies together, mail each other daily and chat on phone.

'Somu! With whom are you talking to so late at night?' Mom had been suspecting it for some time. But I'm her son and born smart.

'It's Paramjeet, Mom!' I then put the call on the loudspeaker. 'Pogo, say hello. Mom thinks that I'm talking to a girl.'

'Hello Aunty,' He would then say.

'Oh! Sorry *beta*,' she would feel really embarrassed. I knew she would never understand, let alone doubt my relation with Pogo.

ॐ

I didn't know how to react on the news, there was just one other instance like that in my life when Danny had offered me the album. The former had brought happiness and the later brought in tears. Pogo was having an arranged marriage and he called to meet me before leaving for his native place. We converged in Ice & Spice.

'Congrats, buddy!' The compliments were not real though.

'Thank you.'

'The beer is on me today.'

'Why? The treat should be on me. I'm getting married.'

'Because I won, I have changed your perspective. I always knew that was going to happen.'

'Really? You would be the same old social jerk. You should have given it a chance.'

'What if I give the chance now? Would you scrap your marriage plans?'

'Well, I would say yes.'

'Think of all the people eagerly awaiting your marriage, your parents and relatives. And, what about that girl? At least, think of her.'

'Why should I? I haven't seen her even once, it's gonna be a blind match.'

'Why are you so bothered about that fact? You only say *na* that love is blind, I teased.'

'Being in my company, you too have learnt to churn out. C'mon, Sam! Say it once that you did care, just once ... nothing is going to change. You see, I am still going to marry that unknown varmint. Please, say it once for me.'

'Of course I did, I do and will always be doing it. But I just care for you as a very close friend of mine.'

'Okay, I give up. I have to go now, have to do some packing.'

'So, see you then. I wish you a very happy married life. Good bye.'

'What? Are you not going to come?'

I smiled and shook my head.

There was both smile on my face and tears in my eyes that night as I lay on my bed, thinking of whatever was happening. Probably, I was missing him. And, I was smiling, because I too had realised that love is blind and yes, it is blind enough not to be able to differentiate between the sexes even. I thought I was going mad. And, it never ends and stays forever. But still I was confused about the physical part. Is it really necessary between two persons in love? I mean we never felt the need for it; perhaps, we enjoyed gaping at the girls together! Oh, we two had such fun.

Damn! Was I upset that Pogo was getting married to someone else? No way, wake up, Sam, my inner voice warned me. The love was more than what I was trying to deduce. With him, I always felt complete; I needed nobody else in my life. He fit in every role. But what about my other desires? So, finally I concluded my love for him—platonic, nothing more than that.

But such relationship could never be understood and are always looked down upon as sin by our society. People are still narrow-minded to accept such ideology. So, it was good for us too, that we didn't get carried away with our relationship because we just could not bear being isolated by the society. Pogo had already taken the initiative and it was my turn to move on. But then, why was I not able to move on. Was it Pogo or was it Shamita. Yes, it was Shamita, she hurt me. Will I ever be able to trust girls now? Why not, that girl just meant sex for me and the other flings I had … I didn't love any of them, they were just to satisfy my lust. I pacified myself and tried to reason with myself. I logged on to orkut …

Me: hi u der?

Maggie: of course, s alwys

Me: So wassup

Maggie: Me just F9 … lemme tel u dat I'm so happy dat v r frens

Me: k den make urself more happy by being my gf
Maggie: Wat?
Me: b my gf
Maggie: R u kidding
Me: nopes I m serious
U said u've a crush on me
Maggie: so
Me: don u luv me
Maggie: dunno
V nvr met each other
Me: k den v meet tomo
Give me a call at 9860000173 at 7.30 eve.
Maggie: r u crazy?
(I didn't reply)

And, that's how I reached Hyderabad. I know it was really a crazy thing to do, but I didn't care. In fact, I thought that there wasn't any harm in meeting her once and who knows, she must be much better than all my girlfriends put together. But that was being really selfish, I knew. I guess that is what life is all about.

I kept the trip as a low profile weekend and so was staying at Hotel Rajdhani in the outer part of the city. Considering the fact that people down here cannot just get over the films by superstars Chiranjeevi or Rajnikant, my music had not reached their ears and I was not recognised at all anywhere. I was contemplating whether she would ever turn up or not because it was already 8.00 and she had yet not called.

'Hey! What's up?' that was Shalini.
'Why have you called now?'
'What happened to you?'
'Nothing, just shoot your problem!'
'Problem? Where are you actually?'

'Don't ask me anything, please!' I urged.

'Okay! Okay! I heard that Pogo is getting married, and thought of giving him a surprise visit. What say?'

'No way dear, I am in Hyderabad.'

'Hyderabad! What are you doing there?'

'Well, I am getting married too.'

'What ... With whom ... But why?' She threw in a number of questions.

I cut her call not because I didn't want to talk to her but I was getting an indication of a call waiting. I had a gut feeling that it was Maggie.

'Hello! Who is it?'

'Hi! It's Maggie,' she really had a damn sweet voice.

'Yeah! it's Hotel Rajdhani ... the address is right ... I will wait for you in the lobby.' I confirmed the address and hung up.

I went downstairs, the lobby was comparatively crowdy and noisy with a few young boys and girls. I hid myself behind the newspaper, to avoid them. I checked the time ... it was already half an hour and still there was no sign of her. The lobby was empty in another minute with just me and the receptionist.

'Well ...', I inquired.

'Yes Sir'.

'I am expecting somebody. Please, send her to Room 307, I will be waiting there.'

'Okay sir! Can you please tell me the name of the visitor?'

'Yeah ... her name is Maggie.'

'What?' The receptionist gave me such a surprised look as if I had said Osama bin Laden.

'Her name is Maggie ...'

'It's Nandini Mehra.' Somebody prompted from the back. I turned around; it was a lady wearing a brown sleeveless T and a knee length denim skirt. I scanned on her other features which were attractive too. She was fair and pretty with a slim figure. She had an oval face with brown eyes and waist length hair. The pleasant smile on her face had raised the testosterone levels in my blood. In one word, she was hot and sexy.

'Maggie?' I asked, I could not believe. Wow … God could be so generous on me, thank you God!

She nodded.

'My name is Nandini.'

I returned her a doubtful look.

'Remember my name. You'll be screaming it later tonight.'

I love you too

Pogo had returned after his marriage and so had I from Hyderabad. He was planning a grand reception and lots of his relatives were to come. He had asked for Amey's flat to use for some time and had called me to help. It was the first time that we were going to meet after his wedding.

I had reached early and was waiting for him to come. I had so many things to share with him; past few days had really been difficult for me. Those hurdles, failures and challenges had made me strong and smart. Most importantly, it taught me to take my own decisions.

'Hi!' Pogo came in finally.

'Looking good, is that the effect of marriage?' I teased.

'Shut up!'

'Okay! Tell me, how is she? And, what's her name actually?'

'Her name is Pammi. Actually, you would laugh at it but her real name is Paramjeet! So, they call me Jeet and her Pammi.'

'How is that possible?'

'It's really common in Punjab. Nothing unusual. Anyway, tell me about your girl.'

'I told you about her. Her name is Nandini. Maggie was just her Orkut username.'

'But that was really crazy from your side. I couldn't believe first when you messaged me about your going to Hyderabad.'

'It was really a crazy thing to do and guess what ... Mom had almost caught me with her. I tell you sometimes Shalini is such a pain in the ass,' I told Pogo everything about my Hyderabad adventure. He was rolling on the floor laughing.

'Nandini is really a good girl. That day when I was out with her, I felt the real essence of true love. We were together all day; we met for lunch, did some shopping, saw a movie and also had a look around the city. Being with her, the feeling dawned on me that she is the one for me.'

'Wow! That's cool. You fell in love once again and I am sure that you gonna be falling in love with someone else again in a few days to come,' Pogo taunted. But that was true; Nandini was the fifth girl in my life, barring my virtual crushes.

'Not this time dude, enough of wandering! I want to settle down. She loves me very much and I feel the same for her. I proposed her before coming back and she said "yes". I want to tell about her to Mom too but then what to do *Mom says no Girlfriend*,' I grinned.

'Then what about a boyfriend?' Pogo paused. 'I still love you.'

'Please! Now don't start it all over again. You're married now!'

'So what? I know with all my heart, there's always enough love for both of you,' he smiled.

'That's really mean to say! Anyway, I've told you about that guy Subho who just barged in when I was with Nandini. He is an author and I've promised him a story. I want everyone to know about our story, our rivalry, our adventures, our friendship, our failures, our success, and the girls and also about my Mom'.

Once again, the hysterical laughter floated around the room recalling my Mom's part.

'But then, your society will come to know everything of our relationship which you always feared.'

'Oh! He's not going to use real names. Anyway, why the hell are you worrying? Hardly, anybody remembers any footballer's name.'

'Okay *baba*, Sam—the great rock star! What about the ending? Is it going to be a happy one?' He said looking at me.

There was something special and different about that stare, I could not hide my feelings anymore. And, finally I said ...

'Pogo! I love you, too.'

www.ingramcontent.com/pod-product-compliance
Lightning Source LLC
Chambersburg PA
CBHW031311150426
43191CB00005B/178